(2002)

£4

Trad

17/06

"WE'LL MEET AGAIN"

SONGS & MUSIC
That Inspired Courage During
WARTIME

Olivia Bailey

Published in 2002 by Caxton Editions
20 Bloomsbury Street
London WC1B 3JH
a member of the Caxton Publishing Group

© 2002 Caxton Publishing Group

Designed and produced for Caxton Editions
by Open Door Limited
Langham, Rutland
Editing: Mary Morton
Colour Separation: GA Graphics, Stamford, UK

Title: "We'll Meet Again": Songs & Music That Inspired Courage During Wartime
ISBN: 1 84067 469 5

"WE'LL MEET AGAIN"

SONGS & MUSIC

That Inspired Courage During

WARTIME

Olivia Bailey

CAXTON EDITIONS

Preface

The history of the world is the history of warfare and this warfare for countless generations has been followed by music. Musicians and bands have always followed troops into battle to inspire them to perform great and heroic deeds. This book looks at the popular music that was inspired by the Great War (World War I) and World War II. The popular music of these times was a great comfort to many people in many different situations. The songs had the power to invoke emotion to make you feel sad, proud, defiant or happy depending on your circumstance. Many of the songs that became famous during World War II had already been made popular during World War I, such as , 'Rule Britannia' and 'Pack Up Your Troubles in Your Old Kit Bag', as well as songs vilifying the enemy. Some of the songs were also taken from the enemy, such as 'Lili Marlene', and then translated in order to boost morale amongst our own troops and as a propaganda move against the enemy.

Music was one of the great escapes during these wars both for the men on the frontline and their families left behind at home. These popular songs helped the troops forget the hardship of war and for a moment at least the gloom and danger, the loneliness and isolation were kept at bay. Dance halls were filled with more people than ever before. Alongside the romance and sentimentality, humour and sarcasm were the ammunition of the British people, helping them to keep stiff upper lips during their darkest hours. Songs and musical comic turns performed in the music halls by favourite entertainers were crucial in sustaining high morale. During World War II ENSA was formed by the Government in order to entertain the troops and the BBC ensured that the music was delivered to the whole world. For the generations who lived through these wars it will bring back memories and for the rest of us it will remind us of an era of great courage.

Bless 'em All!

Contents

World War I
THE GREAT WAR 1914-1918

KEEP THE HOME FIRES BURNING

Words: Lena Guilbert Ford
Music: Ivor Novello.

They were summoned from the hillside,
They were summoned from the glen,
And the country found them ready
At the stirring call for men.

Let no tears add to their hardship,
As the soldiers pass along,
And although your heart is breaking
Make it sing this cheery song.

Keep the home fires burning
While your hearts are yearning,
Though your lads are far away
They dream of home,

There's a silver lining
Through the dark clouds shining.
Turn the dark clouds inside out,
Till the boys come home.

Overseas, there came a pleading:
"Help a nation in distress!"
and we gave our glorious laddies.
Honour bade us do no less.

For no gallant son of Britain
To a foreign yoke shall bend,
And no Englishman is silent
To the sacred call of friend.

The Great War Begins

On the morning of 28 June 1914, the Austrian Archduke Franz Ferdinand and his wife Sophie were assassinated by a member of the Black Hand, a Serbian nationalist organisation, while travelling in a motorcade through Sarajevo, the capital city of Bosnia and Herzegovina. The Archduke had ignored warnings of a possible assassination plot and decided to tour the capital on the anniversary of the 1389 Battle of Kosovo. This battle was a humiliating collective memory for all Serbs, in which Serbia was defeated by the Turks, ending Serbia's independence as a nation.

The Archduke was chosen as a target because Serbians feared that, after his ascension to the throne, he would continue and even heighten the persecution of Serbs living within the Austro-Hungarian empire. Serbia had gained independence from the Ottoman Empire in 1878. At that time, Serbia laid claim to several regions of Bosnia and Herzegovina which were inhabited primarily by Serbs. However, the Congress of Berlin granted permission to Austria-Hungary to occupy Bosnia and Herzegovina, including the disputed Serbian areas. Austria-Hungary officially annexed all of occupied Bosnia and Herzegovina, adding additional fuel to the fire of Serbian nationalism.

Austrian reaction to the assassination was swift, as the Sarajevo crisis was seen as the Empire's last chance to assert its supremacy in the Balkans. Count Leopold von Berchtold, the Austrian foreign minister, was determined to make use of the assassinations to crush once and for all the Serbian nationalist movement. He sent an envoy to Berlin, who was assured by Emperor Wilhelm II on 5 July that Germany would fully support any action which the Dual Monarchy might take against Serbia. On 6 July, the German chancellor Theobold von Bethmann-Hollweg gave his unconditional German support.

7

Above: Archduke Franz Ferdinand and his wife Sophie shortly before their assasination.

On 23 July 1914, Austria-Hungary presented Serbia with a lengthy list of demands, with a 48-hour compliance period, including the abolishment of all Pan-Serb propaganda, expelling from office any persons thought to have nationalist sympathies, taking legal action against certain officials designated by Austria-Hungary, and allowing agents of the Dual Monarchy to control all investigations and proceedings concerning the Sarajevo murders. Minutes before the deadline, Serbia issued a conciliatory reply to Berchtold's demands, stating that Serbia wished the dispute to be submitted to the International Tribunal at the Hague. This conciliation was rejected. On 28 July 1914, Austria-Hungary declared war on Serbia. World War I had begun.

Austria, determined to stifle Serbian aspirations for independence, started to tread on Russian toes in the Balkans; France still burned to avenge the loss of Alsace and Lorraine to Prussia over 40 years before. A test mobilisation of the British Army's 2nd Division took place on 27 July, and by then Winston Churchill had ordered the Grand Fleet to remain in a state of war readiness after the Spithead Review ended. Two days later the War Office sent the order that placed Britain on a war footing. Germany was recalling her officers from leave and within a day was mobilising her forces.

It took little more than a week before more than 80,000 men, their vehicles, horses, ammunition and equipment had joined the advanced parties in France. Commandeered trains took reservists to their battalions and their battalions to the ports. From there they sailed to Boulogne, to Rouen and to Le Havre. They sailed in merchant ships and on cross-channel ferries. For the most part, they sailed by night. Sir John French was given command of this "contemptible little army". Under him were two Corps Commanders – Sir Douglas Haig and Sir James Grierson. French was a dapper man with an eye for the ladies. Haig, commanding the Ist Corps, was taciturn and distant. Grierson's command was brief – after a fatal heart attack at Amiens, Sir Horace Smith-Dorrien took over.

Once they had arrived in France, the British were moved towards the Belgian frontier. Originally joint discussions had decided that the British Expeditionary Force should assemble round Le Cateau and Maubeuge, then take a position on the French left wing, protecting the flank, while the main action of the Franco/German war was fought out in Alsace and Lorraine. Now that Belgium had been invaded, and in spite of French assertions that it was a feint, the British War Office realised that if the Germans invaded France through Belgium, General Lanrezac's Fifth Army could well be swept aside, and only a fractional alteration of course would be needed for von Kluck's First Army to encircle the BEF and destroy it. By now it was too late for the plans to be changed and Britain was now firmly committed.

Lord Kitchener

At the outbreak of World War I, the British Government immediately appointed Lord Kitchener Secretary of State for War. His duties involved the administration of all the British forces, thus troops were efficiently mobilised and generally the people of the country became confident, knowing that such a great commander was overseeing their war effort. His face, with its distinctive handlebar moustache, steely gaze and pointing finger, was also used on the recruiting poster which spoke directly to British men to join the "New Army". Lord Kitchener was then charged with improving the work rate of Britain's industries. He didn't like the job; to him it had little to do with the actual war. Inevitably, he fell out with many of his colleagues – partly also because he was used to being in sole charge of operations.

BRITONS

"WANTS YOU"

JOIN YOUR COUNTRY'S ARMY!
GOD SAVE THE KING

Kitchener died in 1916, when the Russian-bound cruiser he was sailing on was sunk by a German mine.

Above: The famous recruitment poster.

Songs and Bayonets

Song played an almost legendary part in World War I. The Germans invariably came out singing 'Deutschland, Deutschland über Alles', but our men sang to good purpose too. Here is a wonderful picture of the way the Irish Guards met a charge of three German cavalry regiments:

"Rising from the ranks of the Irish, just before the crash came, there reached them the strains of songs they had never heard before. A French soldier, hobbling along with a bandaged face and a bullet in his back, ventured to repeat from memory the beginnings of a tune which I made out to be that of 'God Save Ireland', and 'I Have Gathered that Whistle to Me, Said I' was another of these strains."

The storyteller then heard the almost legendary 'It's a Long, Long Way to Tipperary', a song originally introduced by the Connaught Rangers and sung by marching soldiers ever since.

IT'S A LONG, LONG WAY TO TIPPERARY

Written by Jack Judge and Harry Williams

It's a long way to Tipperary.
It's a long way to go.

It's a long way to Tipperary
To the sweetest girl I know!

Goodbye Piccadilly.
Farewell, Leicester Square,

It's a long, long way to Tipperary,
But my heart's right there!

The gramophone was played in the trenches, too, and there are innumerable references to the pleasure it gave the troops. An eye-witness tells how one instrument not only gave a concert in the British camp itself, but also played to the men many miles away in the rifle-pits, the melodies being passed to them by means of an electrophone. The Germans used gramophones and the French had them, too, though they sometimes employed them as an instrument of war. One was placed well away from a trench, fitted with a record of the 'Marseillaise' and wound up. Provoked by this, a number of hidden Germans started to blast away at the gramophone – which is what the French soldiers wanted.

Having found their enemy's position by gramophone, the French then proceeded to exterminate them by fire.

'Bombed Last Night' is typical of much trench music. Firstly, it was sung as a chant, enabling soldiers of all vocal abilities to join in. Secondly, it relied on repetition and imagination on the soldiers' behalf. This meant that one soldier could "lead", making up the lyrics, while everyone else could then accompany him. Other verses included "Drunk last night" and "Shelled last night".

BOMBED LAST NIGHT

From the trenches 1917

Bombed last night,
and bombed the night before.
Going to get bombed
tonight if we never get bombed anymore.

When we're bombed,
we're scared as we can be.
Can't stop the bombing
from old Higher Germany.

They're warning us, they're warning us.
One shell hole for just the four of us.
Thank your lucky stars
there are no more of us.
So one of us can fill it all alone.

Gassed last night, and gassed
the night before.
Going to get gassed tonight if we
never get gassed anymore.

When we're gassed,
we're sick as we can be.
For phosgene and mustard gas is much
too much for me.

They're killing us, they're killing us.
One respirator for the four of us.
Thank your lucky stars
that we can all run fast.
So one of us can take it all alone.

11 *Above: Soldiers in the trenches during World War II.*

Other times the men would sing a haunting song of longing such as 'I Want To Go Home'.

Taken from the music-hall song 'On Sunday I Walk Out With a Sailor', this song converts recruitment propaganda into intensely resentful verse. The "lady whore" is usually edited into a "well paid lady", or "a lady typist", an indication of how the soldiers' versions were cleaned up for a civilian audience.

Piccadilly Circus was known at this time for the high percentage of prostitutes, tramps and pimps who frequented the area. Back home in "Blighty" the theatres and music halls were packed out with soldiers, and their girls, waiting to go off to the front. Both the London theatres and the music halls saw a huge rise in ticket sales with many patriotic songs inspiring their audiences. 'Keep the Home Fires Burning' captured the mood of the time and is still very popular today. It was written by a young Welshman named Ivor Novello

I WANT TO GO HOME

I want to go home, I want to go home.
I don't want to go in the trenches no more,
Where whizzbangs and shrapnel they whistle and roar.
Take me over the sea,
where the alleyman can't get at me.

Oh my, I don't want to die,
I want to go home.

I want to go home, I want to go home.
I don't want to visit la Belle France no more,
For oh the Jack Johnsons they make such a roar.
Take me over the sea,
where the snipers they can't get at me.

Oh my, I don't want to die,
I want to go home.

Ivor Novello

Ivor Novello was born in Cardiff and educated at Magdalen College School, Oxford where he was a chorister. His song, 'Keep the Home Fires Burning' was one of the most successful of World War I. Many other songs, among them 'Dreamboat' and 'We'll Gather Lilacs' followed, making him one of the most successful songwriters of his day. By 1921 he was appearing on stage in London enjoying immense popularity.

In 1924 he wrote his first play, *The Rat*, in collaboration with Constance Collier. He often played the leading role in the predominantly melodramatic, romantic musicals that he wrote. Amongst his successes were *Symphony in Two Flats* (1930), *The Truth Game* (1934), *Proscenium* (1934), *Glamorous Nights* (1935), *Careless Rapture* (1936), *Full House* (1936), *Comedienne* (1938), *The Dancing Years* (1939), *Perchance To Dream* (1945), *We Proudly Present* (1947) and *King's Rhapsody* (1949). The music was sentimental with very gentle plotlines.

Although Novello was openly homosexual, by taking the non-singing lead in his shows, he built a great following with the female audience. Novello's shows also helped fill London's theatre during World War II. He continued to produce new plays like *Arc de Triomphe* and *Gay's the Word*.

WE'LL GATHER LILACS

Ivor Novello

We'll gather lilacs in the spring again

And walk together down an English lane,
Until our hearts have learned to sing again,

When you come home once more.

And in the evening by the firelight's glow,
You'll hold me close and never let me go.

Your eyes will tell me all I want to know,
When you come home once more.

And in the evening by the firelight's glow,
You'll hold me close and never let me go.

Your eyes will tell me all I want to know,
When you come home once more.

13

Above: Ivor Novello.

WORLD WAR I – THE GREAT WAR 1914-1918

During 1914 the theatres and music halls in London were putting on the following shows:

TITLE	VENUE
Adele	Gaiety
After the Girl	Gaiety
The Belle of Bond Street	Gaiety
Business As Usual	Hippodrome
By Jingo – If We Do	Hippodrome
The Cinema Star	Shaftesbury
The Cockyolly Bird	Shaftesbury
Little Dora's Doze	Shaftesbury
Happy Days	Shaftesbury
Honeymoon Express	Shaftesbury
Mam'selle Tra-La-La	Lyric
A Mixed Grill	Lyric
Not Likely	Lyric
On Duty	Lyric
The Passing Show	Palace

Christmas Truce

On 7 December 1914, there was an informal break in the hostilities for the celebration of Christmas.

Even without an official cessation of war for Christmas, family and friends of the soldiers wanted to make their loved ones' Christmas special. They sent packages filled with letters, warm clothing, food, cigarettes and medications. The presence of small Christmas trees made it extra special.

On Christmas Eve, many German soldiers put up their Christmas trees, decorated with candles, on the parapets of their trenches. Hundreds of Christmas trees lighted the German trenches. The British soldiers could see the lights but it took them a few minutes to figure out what they were from. British lookouts reported the phenomenon to their superiors. British soldiers were ordered not to fire but to watch them closely. Then the British soldiers heard the Germans singing.

During the course of Christmas Eve, there wafted from the German trenches the sounds of celebrating and merry-making, and occasionally the guttural tones of a German were to be heard shouting out lustily, "A happy Christmas to you Englishmen!" Only too glad to show that the sentiments were reciprocated, the English responded in turn. In other areas, the two sides exchanged Christmas carols.

15

Above: Drawing of the Christmas truce from the British "Sphere" magazine.

"They finished their carol and we thought that we ought to retaliate in some way, so we sang 'The first Noël', and when we finished that they all began clapping; and then they struck up another favourite of theirs, 'O Tannenbaum'. And so it went on. First the Germans would sing one of their carols and then we would sing one of ours, until when we started up 'O Come All Ye Faithful' the Germans immediately joined in singing the same hymn to the Latin words 'Adeste Fideles'."

The fraternisation on both Christmas Eve and Christmas Day was in no way officially sanctioned nor organised. Yet, in numerous separate instances along the front line, German soldiers began yelling over to their enemy, "Tommy, you come over and see us!". Still cautious, the British soldiers would rally back, "No, you come here!"

In some parts of the line, representatives of each side met in the middle, in No Man's Land, shook hands, wished each other a Merry Christmas and were soon conversing as if they had known each other for years. Some of those who went out to meet the enemy in the middle of No Man's Land on Christmas Eve or on Christmas Day negotiated a truce: "We won't fire if you won't fire". Some ended the truce at midnight on Christmas night, some extended it until New Year's Day.

One of the main reasons Christmas truces were negotiated was in order to bury the dead. Though some had died recently, there were corpses out in No Man's Land that had been there for several months. Along with the revelry that accompanied Christmas was the sad and sombre job of burying their fallen comrades. On Christmas Day, British and German soldiers appeared on No Man's Land and sorted through the bodies. In a few rare instances, joint services were held for both the British and German dead.

Yet many soldiers enjoyed meeting the unseen enemy and were surprised to discover that they were more alike than they had thought. They talked, shared pictures, exchanged items such as buttons or helmets for foodstuffs. An extreme example of the fraternisation was a soccer game played in the middle of No Man's Land between the Bedfordshire Regiment and the Germans. A member of the Bedfordshire Regiment produced a ball and the large group of soldiers played until the ball was deflated when it hit a barbed wire entanglement.

This strange and unofficial truce lasted for several days, much to the dismay of the commanding officers. This amazing display of Christmas cheer was never again repeated and, as World War I progressed, the story of Christmas 1914 at the front became something of a legend.

O COME ALL YE FAITHFUL

Words and music by John F. Wade

O come all ye faithful,
Joyful and triumphant,
O come ye, O come ye to Bethlehem.
Come and behold him,
Born the king of angels:

O come, let us adore him,
O come, let us adore him,
O come, let us adore him,
Christ the Lord.

Sing, choirs of angels,
sing in exultation,
sing all ye citizens of
heaven above.
Glory to God
in the highest:

O come, let us adore him,
O come, let us adore him,
O come, let us adore him,
Christ the Lord.

Yea, Lord we greet thee,
Born this happy morning,
Jesu, to thee be all glory given;
Word of the Father,
Now in flesh appearing:

O come, let us adore him,
O come, let us adore him,
O come, let us adore him,
Christ the Lord.

O TANNENBAUM (OH CHRISTMAS TREE)

O Christmas tree, O Christmas tree!
How are thy leaves so verdant!
O Christmas tree,
O Christmas tree,
How are thy leaves so verdant!

For every year the Christmas tree,
Brings to us all both joy and glee.
O Christmas tree,
O Christmas tree,
Much pleasure doth thou bring me!

Not only in the summertime,
But even in winter is thy prime.
O Christmas tree,
O Christmas tree,
How are thy leaves so verdant!

O Christmas tree,
O Christmas tree,
Thy candles shine out brightly!
O Christmas tree,
O Christmas tree,
Thy candles shine out brightly!

O Christmas tree,
O Christmas tree,
Much pleasure doth
thou bring me!
O Christmas tree,
O Christmas tree,
Much pleasure doth
thou bring me!

WORLD WAR I – THE GREAT WAR 1914-1918

Events of 1914

28 June	Archduke Franz Ferdinand assassinated in Sarajevo.
28 July	Austria-Hungary declares war on Russia.
2 August	Germany invades Luxembourg.
3 August	Germany declares war on France.
4 August	Britain declares war on Germany and Austria-Hungary.
4 August	German forces invade Belgium in violation of a treaty signed by Prussia to respect Belgian neutrality.
19 August	President Wilson appeals for neutrality.
26–30 August	Battle of Tannenberg.
August	Battle of Togoland.
August	Pursuit of the Goeben and the Breslau.
September	First Battle of Aisne.
September	Battle of Lemberg.
5–10 September	First Battle of the Marne.
October–November	First Battle of Ypres.
November	Battle of Lodz.
21 December	First Zeppelin raid on London.
25 December	Unofficial Christmas Truce on the Western Front.

PACK UP YOUR TROUBLES IN YOUR OLD KIT BAG

Written by Felix Powell and George Asaf

Private Perks is a funny little codger
With a smile, a funny smile.
Five foot none, he's an artful dodger
With a smile, a funny smile.
Flush or broke, he'll have his little joke;
he can't be suppressed.
All the other fellows have to grin,
When he get's this off his chest, Hi!

Pack up your troubles in your old kit bag
and smile, smile, smile!
While you've a lucifer to light your fag
Smile, boys, that's the style!
What's the use of worrying?
It never was worth while
So, pack up your troubles in your old kit bag
and smile, smile, smile!

Private Perks went a-marching into Flanders
with a smile, his funny smile.
He was loved by the privates and
commanders for his smile, his funny smile.
When a throng of "Bosches" came along
with a mighty swing
Perks yelled out "This little bunch is mine!
Keep your heads down, boys, and sing! Hi!

Pack up your troubles in your old kit bag
and smile, smile, smile!
While you've a lucifer to light your fag
Smile, boys, that's the style!
What's the use of worrying?
It never was worth while
So, pack up your troubles in your old kit bag
and smile, smile, smile!

Private Perks, he came back from
Bosche shooting
with his smile, his funny smile.
Round his home he then set about recruiting
With his smile, his funny smile.
He told all his pals, the short and the tall,
What a time he'd had
And each enlisted like a man.
Private Perks said "Now my lad" Hi!

Pack up your troubles in your old kit bag
and smile, smile, smile!
While you've a lucifer to light your fag
Smile, boys, that's the style!
What's the use worrying?
It never was worth while
So, pack up your troubles in your old kit bag
and smile, smile, smile!"

Rudyard Kipling's Plea for Bands

Reprinted from *The Times*, London, 28 January 1915:

"Mr Rudyard Kipling delivered an interesting speech yesterday at the Mansion House at a meeting promoted by the Recruiting Bands Committee and held with the object of raising bands in the London district as an aid to recruiting.

"Mr Rudyard Kipling said –

"I am not a musician, so if I speak as a barbarian I must ask you and several gentlemen on the platform here to forgive me. From the lowest point of view, a few drums and fifes in the battalion means at least five extra miles in a route march, quite apart from the fact that they can swing a battalion back to quarters happy and composed in its mind, no matter how wet or tired its body may be. Even when there is no route marching, the mere come and go – the roll and flourishing of drums and fifes around the barracks – is as warming and cheering as the sight of a fire in a room. A band – not necessarily a full band, but a band of a dozen brasses and woodwinds – is immensely valuable in the district where men are billeted. It revives memories, it quickens association, it opens and unites the hearts of men more surely than any other appeal can, and in this respect it aids recruiting perhaps more than any other agency. I wonder whether I should say this – the tunes that it employs and the words that go with that tune are sometimes very remote from heroism or devotion, but the magic and the compelling power is in them, and it makes men's souls realise certain truths that their minds might doubt.

"Further, no one, not even the adjutant can say for certain where the soul of the battalion lives, but the expression of that soul is most often found in the band. [Cheers]. It stands to reason that 1,200 men whose lives are pledged to each other must have some common means of expression, some common means of conveying their moods and their thoughts to themselves and their world. The band feels the moods and interprets the thoughts. A wise and sympathetic bandmaster – and the masters that I have met have been that – can lift a battalion out of depression, cheer it in sickness, and steady and recall it to itself in times of almost unendurable stress.

[Cheers]. I remember in India in a cholera camp, where the men were suffering very badly, the band of the 10th Lincolns started a regimental sing-song and went on with that queer, defiant tune 'The Lincolnshire Poacher'. It was their regimental march that the men had heard a thousand times. There was nothing in it – nothing except all England, all the East Coast, all the fun and daring and horseplay of young men bucketing about big pastures in the moonlight.

21

"But as it was given very softly at that bad time in that terrible camp of death, it was the one thing in the world that could have restored as it did restore shaken men back to their pride, humour, and self-control. [Cheers].

"Sir F. Bridge said that what was wanted was a band that would play good rousing march tunes such as he remembered in Rochester when the 18th Royal Irish were setting out for the Crimean War, after badly damaging six policemen the night before. [Laughter].

"With £1,000 a week they ought to have 20 good bands to provide good old tunes like 'Tipperary', 'Ninety-Five' and 'Rory O'More'."

Above: Kipling believed that a sympathetic bandmaster could lift a battalion out of depression in times of almost unendurable stress.

Concert Parties and Music Hall

In the pre-war era there was a distinct separation between concert parties and music hall. The former involved recitals or demonstrations and was attended by the middle classes. The latter, although immensely popular, was deemed "vulgar" by the middle classes due to the level of familiarity and participation demanded of the audience and so was attended by the working classes only. During the war, because of the cultural circumstances of the troops, the two entertainment forms slowly blended into each other, although this never became established on the home front in the same way.

Concert parties were often performed by well-meaning civilians in local town halls, for the troops still in England, with attendance often being compulsory. Usually they consisted of a series of "turns", involving local talents or interests, and edifying speeches directed at the troops. They were however highly successful and several civilian troupes, including the Young Men's Christian Association and Concerts at the Front, went abroad to entertain the army.

The civilian-organised events were far more civilised affairs, having a strictly middle-class mixture of stirring songs and wordy recitals. However, there was a distinct cultural clash between the civilian idea of the war and the actuality of the war, which the soldiers often found uncomfortable and

23

Above: Rudyard Kipling.

offensive. Indeed divisional performances were far more bawdy and realistic but the troops appreciated this more. By 1915, many divisions had their own troupes who were largely excused from active duty and toured rest areas giving performances.

These included the Follies (4th Division), the Fancies (6th Division) and the Bow Bells (56th Division). The army put considerable work into supporting these events, and frequently commandeered repair parties to erect halls in which to perform behind the lines. Army concert parties had a slightly different structure which overlapped with the themes of music hall.

Music hall was a well established aspect of working-class entertainment but it depended heavily on the audience's participation as well as that of performers. Active participation in frequent asides to the crowd was expected, along with the singing of familiar songs, retelling of popular jokes and comedy sketches. It was this interaction and bawdiness, as well as the images of home it evoked, that ensured its popularity with the troops.

At first the middle-class officers would arrange concert parties for their men, not realising the vast majority of them preferred the music-hall tradition because of their working-class upbringing. Slowly this demand drew the concert parties towards the music-hall style and many of the organised troupes began to use music-hall

themes in their acts. Army music-hall performances featured songs ranging from the highly sentimental to the grossly obscene and sketches included parodies of army life, drag acts, farces and take-offs of famous comedy acts, especially Charlie Chaplin and Harold Lloyd. The songs and skits were often altered to depict aspects of army life and as such could become extremely vulgar or aggressive in content.

Drag acts were very popular, possibly because of the separation from women and also because they satirised elements of home life that the soldiers resented. Satire against the incompetence of generals, the ignorance of the home front and the absurdity of army life were predominant themes in these performances and allowed the soldiers to feel that they were sharing a common experience. However, one subject that was taboo was death, either the act of killing or the mention of casualties, since the shows were designed to boost morale.

There was also a great deal of sentimentality and communal singing of familiar songs, which played on idealised memories of home and the peaceful pre-war era, songs such as the romantic 'Roses of Picardy'. Englishness drew heavily on similar ideologies. The songs helped reinforce a sense of community, increased morale and brought comfort. It also reminded the soldiers that there was a "normal" and stable world back home for them to return to.

ROSES OF PICARDY

*Written by Haydn Wood
and Fred Weatherly*

*Roses are shining in Picardy
In the hush of the silvery dew;
Roses are flowering in Picardy,
But there's never a rose like you,
And the roses will die in
the summer time,
And our roads may be far apart,
But there's one rose that
dies not in Picardy,
That's the rose that I keep in my heart.*

*Roses are shining in Picardy
In the hush of the silvery dew;
Roses are flowering in Picardy,
But there's never a rose like you,
And the roses will die in
the summer time,
And our roads may be far apart,
But there's one rose that
dies not in Picardy,
That's the rose that I keep in my heart.*

During 1915 the theatres and music halls in London were putting on the following shows:

Title	Venue
5064 Gerrard	Alhambra
All Scotch	Alhambra
Betty	Daly's
Bric-a-Brac	Palace
Fads and Fancies	Palace
Joyland	Hippodrome
Keep to the Right	Hippodrome
Looking Around	Garrick
Miss Springtime	Garrick
Now's the Time	Alhambra
The Only Girl	Apollo
The Passing Show of 1915	Palace
Push and Go	Hippodrome
Rosy Rapture, the Pride of the Beauty Chorus	Hippodrome Duke of York's
Samples	Playhouse
Shell Out	Comedy
Tina	Adelphi
Tonight's the Night	Gaiety
Watch Your Step	Gaiety
The Whirl of the Town	Palladium

Above: George Robey.

George Robey, 1869-1954

George Robey began his career as a music-hall singer but was more noted for his acting rather than his singing. The song most closely associated with him, 'If You Were the Only Girl in the World', is a revue rather than a music-hall song. This became enormously popular in the Great War, following his performance of it with Violet Loraine. Robey enjoyed playing with language in the tradition of the hyperbolic chairmen of the old halls. "Kindly temper your hilarity with a modicum of reserve," he would urge his audiences, which would be followed by the blunt "Desist!" He would also switch from mock-elevated speech to slang in his songs.

Robey was a talented man in and out of the theatre. He excelled as an amateur in a number of widely different fields. In his profession he became known as the "Prime Minister of Mirth" and was a magnificent pantomime dame. He also played Shakespeare with success as Falstaff (on the stage in 1935 in *Henry IV, Part I* and in Olivier's film of *Henry V*); in comic opera (as Menelaus in Offenbach's *Helen*); and in films, including that remarkable version of *Don Quixote* directed by Pabst with Chaliapin as the Don and Robey as Sancho Panza. (He had earlier played Sancho Panza in a silent version of *Don Quixote*). In 1954 he was knighted and later that year, he died.

IF YOU WERE THE ONLY GIRL IN THE WORLD

Written by Nat D. Ayer and Clifford Grey

Some times when I feel bad
And things look blue
I wish a pal I had,
Say one like you!
Someone within my heart
To build a throne.
Someone who'd never part,
To call my own.

If you were the only girl in the world,
And I were the only boy,
Nothing else would matter
In the world today.
We could go on loving
In the same old way.

A Garden of Eden
Just made for two,
With nothing
To mar our joy.
I would say such
Wonderful things to you,
There would be such
Wonderful things to do,

If you were the only girl in the world
And I were the only boy.

Events of 1915

19 January	German zeppelin air raid on England.
4 February	Germany declares a submarine blockade of England.
February	Battle of Masuria.
March	Battle of Neuve-Chapelle.
March–December	Battles of Aubers Ridge and Festubert.
22 April–5 May	Second Battle of Ypres. First use of chemical weapons.
23 April	Allied assault on Gallipoli.
7 May	*Lusitania* sunk.
May	Battle of Gorlice-Tarnow.
13 May	First *Lusitania* note to Germany from America.
30 August	Responding to American demands, Germany stops sinking ships without warning.
5 September	Tsar Nicholas commander of Russian armies.
September–October	Battles of Artois and Champagne.
September–October	Battle of Loos.
7 December	David Lloyd George becomes Prime Minister of Britain.
December	Allied withdrawal from Gallipoli.

RULE BRITANNIA

Written by James Thomson

When Britain first, at heaven's command,
Arose from out the azure main;
This was the charter of the land,
And guardian angels sung this strain:

Rule, Britannia, rule the waves;
Britons never will be slaves.

The nations, not so blest as thee,
Must, in their turns, to tyrants fall:
While thou shalt flourish great and free,
The dread and envy of them all.

Still more majestic shalt thou rise,
More dreadful, from each foreign stroke:
As the loud blast that tears the skies,
Serves but to root thy native oak.

Thee haughty tyrants ne'er shall tame:
All their attempts to bend thee down,
Will but arouse thy generous flame;
But work their woe, and thy renown.

To thee belongs the rural reign;
Thy cities shall with commerce shine:
All thine shall be the subject main,
And every shore it circles thine.

The Muses, still with freedom found,
Shall to thy happy coast repair:
Blest isle! with matchless beauty crowned,
And manly hearts to guard the fair.

The Battle of Jutland

During 1916 the war at sea was stepped up. The Battle of Jutland was described by Rudyard Kipling in his series of reports in the London *Daily Telegraph*. For reasons of security he used fictitious names for the destroyers.

"When the German fleet ran for home, on the night of 31 May, it seems to have scattered – 'starred' I believe is the word for the evolution – in a general sauve qui peut, while the Devil, lively represented by our destroyers, took the hindmost. Our flotillas were strung out far and wide on this job. One man compared it to hounds hunting half a hundred separate foxes. I take the adventures of several couples of destroyers who, on the night of 31 May, were nosing along somewhere towards the Schleswig-Holstein coast, ready to chop any Hun stuff coming back to earth by that particular road. The leader of one line was Gehenna, and the next two ships astern of her were Eblis and Shaitan, in the order given ...

Above: Battle of Jutland.

30

"Towards midnight our destroyers were overtaken by several three- and four-funnel German ships (cruisers, they thought) hurrying home. At this stage of the game anybody might have been anybody – pursuer or pursued. The Germans took no chances, but switched on their searchlights and opened fire on Gehenna. Her Acting Sublieutenant reports: 'A salvo hit us forward. I opened fire with the afterguns. A shell then struck us in a steampipe, and I could see nothing but steam. But both starboard torpedoes were fired.'

"Eblis, Gehenna's next astern, at once fired a torpedo at the second ship in the German line, a four-funnelled cruiser, and hit her between the second funnel and the mainmast, when 'she appeared to catch fire fore and aft simultaneously, heeled right over to starboard, and undoubtedly sank.' Eblis loosed off a second torpedo and turned aside to reload, firing at the same time to distract the enemy's attention from Gehenna, who was now ablaze fore and aft. Gehenna's Acting Sublieutenant (the only executive officer who survived) says that by the time the steam from the broken pipe cleared he found Gehenna stopped, nearly everybody amidships killed or wounded, the cartridge boxes round the guns exploding one after the other as the fires took hold, and the enemy not to be seen. Three minutes or less did all that damage.

"Eblis had nearly finished reloading when a shot struck the davit that was swinging her last torpedo into the tube and wounded all hands concerned. Thereupon she dropped torpedo work, fired at an enemy searchlight which winked and went out, and was closing in to help Gehenna, when she found herself under the noses of a couple of enemy cruisers... The enemy did her best. She completely demolished the Eblis's bridge and searchlight platform, brought down the mast and the forefunnel, ruined the whaler and the dinghy, split the foc's'le open above water from the stern to the galley which is abaft the bridge, and below water had opened it up from the stern to the second bulkhead. She further ripped off Eblis's skin plating for an amazing number of yards on one side of her, and fired a couple of large calibre shells into Eblis at point-blank range narrowly missing her vitals. Even so, Eblis is as impartial as a prize court....

"After all that Eblis picked herself up, and discovered that she was still alive, with a dog's chance of getting to port. But she did not bank on it. That grand slam had wrecked the bridge, pinning the commander under the wreckage. By the time he had extricated himself he 'considered it advisable to throw overboard the steel chest and dispatch box of confidential and secret books.' [These] are never allowed to fall into strange hands, and their proper disposal is the last step but one in the ritual of the burial service of His Majesty's ships at sea.

"Gehenna, afire and sinking, out somewhere in the dark, was going through it on her own account. This is her Acting Sublieutenant's report: 'The confidential books were got up. The First Lieutenant gave the order: "Every man aft," and the confidential books were thrown overboard. The ship soon afterwards heeled over to starboard and the bows went under. The First Lieutenant gave the order: "Everybody for themselves." The ship sank in about a minute, the stern going straight up into the air.'

"But it was not written in the Book of Fate that stripped and battered Eblis should die that night as Gehenna died. After the burial of the books it was found that the several fires on her were manageable, that she 'was not making water aft of the damage,' which meant two thirds of her were, more or less, in commission, and, best of all, that three boilers were usable in spite of the cruiser's shells. So she 'shaped course and speed to make the least water and the most progress towards land.'

"On the way back the wind shifted eight points without warning – and, what with one thing and another, Eblis was unable to make any port till the scandalously late hour of noon 2 June, 'the mutual ramming having occurred about 11:40 P.M. on 31 May.' She says, this time without any legal reservation whatever, "I cannot speak too highly of the courage, discipline, and devotion of the officers and ship's company.

"In that flotilla alone there was every variety of fight, from the ordered attacks of squadrons under control, to single ship affairs, every turn of which depended on the second's decision of the men concerned; endurance to the hopeless end; bluff and cunning; reckless advance and redhot flight; clear vision and as much of blank bewilderment as the Senior Service permits its children to indulge in. That is not much. When a destroyer who has been dodging enemy torpedoes and gunfire in the dark realizes about midnight that she is 'following a strange British flotilla, having lost sight of my own,' she 'decides to remain with them,' and shares their fortunes and whatever language is going.

"If lost hounds could speak when they cast up next day, after an unchecked night among the wild life of the dark, they would talk much as our destroyers do."

The Royal Navy had its fair share of songs, too.

'Fire Down Below' was used as a pumping shanty. When wooden ships were replaced by iron ships, the shanty was used for the capstan. It was one of the last shanties sung aboard the British squarerigger *Garthpool* just before it wrecked on Ponta Reef, Cape Verde Islands in October 1929.

FIRE DOWN BELOW

Written by Lesley Nelson-Burns

Fire in the galley, fire in the house,
Fire in the beef kid, scorching the scouse.
Fire, fire, fire down below.
Fetch a bucket of water,
Fire down below.

Fire in the cabin, fire in the hold,
Fire in the strong room melting the gold.
Fire, fire, fire down below.
Fetch a bucket of water,
Fire down below.

Fire round the capstan, fire on the mast,
Fire on the main deck, burning it fast.
Fire, fire, fire down below.
Fetch a bucket of water,
Fire down below.

Fire in the lifeboat, fire in the gig,
Fire in the pig-sty roasting the pig.
Fire, fire, fire down below.
Fetch a bucket of water,
Fire down below.

Fire in the store room spoiling the food,
Fire on the orlop burning the wood.
Fire, fire, fire down below.
Fetch a bucket of water,
Fire down below.

Fire on the waters, fire high above,
Fire in our hearts for the friends that we love.
Fire, fire, fire down below.
Fetch a bucket of water,
Fire down below.

A "beef kid" is a small wooden tub in which beef salt is served. "Scouse" is a mixture of salt, beef and crushed biscuit and the "orlop" is a lower deck.

Many of the naval songs feature the ship-
building tree of England, the oak.

HEARTS OF OAK

Come cheer up, my lads!
'tis to glory we steer,
To add something more
to this wonderful year;
To honour we call you,
not press you like slaves,
For who are so free as the
sons of the waves?

Chorus

Heart of oak are our ships,
heart of oak are our men;
We always are ready,
steady, boys, steady!
We'll fight and we'll conquer
again and again.

We ne'er see our foes
but we wish them to stay.
They never see us but they wish us away;
If they run, why we follow,
and run them ashore,
For if they won't fight us,
we cannot do more.

Chorus

They swear they'll invade us,
these terrible foes,
They frighten our women,
our children, and beaus;
But should their flat bottoms
in darkness get o'er,
Still Britons they'll find to receive
them on shore.

Chorus

We'll still make them fear,
and we'll still make them flee,
And drub 'em on shore,
as we've drubb'd 'em at sea;
Then cheer up, my lads!
with one heart let us sing:
Our soldiers, our sailors,
our statesmen and King.

During 1916 the theatres and music halls in London were putting on the following shows:

Title	Venue
The Bing Boys Are Here	Alhambra
Blighty	Oxford
Flying Colours	Hippodrome
Follow the Crowd	Empire
Half-Past Eight	Comedy
The Happy Day	Daly's
High Jinks	Adelphi
Houp-la	St Martin's
Look Who's Here	London Opera House
Mr Manhattan	Prince of Wales
My Lady Frayle	Shaftesbury
Pell-Mell	Ambassador
Razzle-Dazzle	Theatre Royal, Drury Lane
See-Saw	Comedy
Some	Vaudeville
Theodore & Co	Gaiety
This and That	
Three Cheers	Shaftesbury
Toto	Duke of York's
Vanity Fair	Palace
We're All In It	Empire
Young England	Daly's

Harry Lauder, 1870-1950

Henry MacLennan Lauder, called Harry, was the first of eight children born to John and Isabella MacLennan Lauder. Harry's father died of pneumonia when Harry was 12 and he was forced into working part-time in a flax mill to help his mother support his younger siblings. Attending school three days a week, he delighted in entertaining his class-mates with imitations of their teacher. Two years later Harry found work in a coal mine. It was dangerous work and he sang to himself to bolster his courage. His co-workers encouraged him to enter local talent contests that earned small but cherished prize money. He finally entered a contest singing the two songs he knew best, 'Bonnie Annie Laurie' and 'I'm a Gentleman Still'.

I'M A GENTLEMAN STILL

Though poverty daily looks in at my door,
Though I'm hungry and footsore and ill,
Thank God, I can look the whole world in the face
And say, I'm a gentleman still!

35

Above: Harry Lauder.

He won second prize and was given the chance to sing in small local music halls. He soon rose to fame. Harry met Annie Valance, destined to be the only woman he would ever love; it was love at first sight and he could think of nothing or no one else. Though still teenagers, they gained family permission to marry. He wrote 'I love a Lassie', 'She is my Rosie', 'Queen Among the Heather', 'She's the Lass for Me' and 'Bonnie Wee Annie' all for his "Nance" a nickname that he gave her.

Above: Harry Lauder began singing when he worked down the coal mines, to lift his spirit and bolster his courage.

When Harry Lauder visited his son Captain John Lauder prior to his posting overseas he asked every soldier that he met: "What can I get for you? What do you need?" The answer was nearly always the same: "More men." At his own expense Harry Lauder hired one hundred pipers to march the length and breadth of Scotland to recruit men – which, it is said, is why the bulk of the British forces in WWI were Scots. The enemy called the Scottish troops, "The Ladies From Hell" wearing their kilts, brandishing their bayonets and shouting gaelic war cries.

Toward the end of the war he kept seeing wounded and disabled soldiers in the hospitals. He knew that they would receive a government allowance but he also knew it wasn't enough for them to support themselves. He did not want them to become objects of charity or reduced to selling matches on a street corner. He used his performances to create a fund to ensure that these men would have what they needed to live the dignified life they had earned for King and Country.

On 1 January 1916, while Harry was on tour, he received a telegram. It read, "Captain John Lauder killed in action 28 December 1915". Harry Lauder and his beloved wife Nance had lost their only child on a battlefield in France. The theatre manager closed the show until further notice knowing it would be impossible for Harry to go on stage to tell jokes and sing.

Harry rushed home to be with his wife and spend a private time of grief and prayer. His wife reminded him of the millions of other parents that had received similar telegrams and encouraged him to go back to London and reopen the show to prevent the laying-off of hundreds of people. Returning to the theatre, Harry was given a letter that had arrived by special messenger. It was from a fellow officer who had been with his son John when he was killed. "The Captain", he wrote, had "died with great gallantry calling out the words 'Carry on'." Harry Lauder, distraught, answered his dying son in the only way he knew – and thus the maxim of entertainers that "the show must go on" was born. Harry, did carry on that night singing his songs and telling jokes, giving all he had to give. When the final curtain came down he fainted.

Weeks later he tried to enlist for combat and was rejected because of his age. He then asked to go overseas to entertain at the front. No one had ever made such a request before. Many performers had entertained in military hospitals, but none had actually gone to the battlefield. After weeks of debate in the War Office Harry Lauder became the first person to entertain troops (both British and American) on the battlefield.

With a small custom-built piano tied to the grille of a military vehicle he sang and joked his way across France in base hospitals, old chateaux, pillaged barns and dug-outs. It was a practice he repeated in World War II at the personal request of Sir Winston Churchill.

His Majesty King George V bestowed a knighthood on Harry Lauder for service to his country after the Great War.

Above: Winston Churchill personally requested the talents of Harry Lauder in World War II, after his success as a moral booster in World War I.

I LOVE A LASSIE

I love a lassie, a bonnie Hielan' lassie,
If you saw her you would fancy her as well:
I met her in September, popped the
question in November,
So I'll soon be havin' her a' to ma-sel'.
Her faither has consented,
so I'm feelin' quite contented
'Cause I've been and sealed
the bargain wi' a kiss.
I sit and weary, weary,
when I think aboot ma deary,
An' you'll always hear me singing this.

Chorus

I love a lassie, a bonnie, bonnie lassie,
She's as pure as a lily in the dell,
She's sweet as the heather, the bonnie
bloomin' heather,
Mary, my Scots bluebell.

I love a lassie, a bonnie Hielan' lassie,
She can warble like a
blackbird in the dell.
She's an angel ev'ry Sunday,
but a jolly lass on Monday:
She's as modest as her namesake the bluebell.
She's nice, she's neat,
she's tidy and I meet her ev'ry Friday:
That's a special nicht, you bet,
I never miss.

I'm enchanted, I'm enraptured,
since ma heart the darlin' captur'd,
She's intoxicated me with bliss.

Chorus

I love a lassie, a bonnie Hielan' lassie,
I could sit an' let her tease me for a week:
For the way she keeps behavin'
well, I never pay for shavin',
'Cause she rubs ma whiskers
clean off with her cheek.
And underneath ma bonnet,
where the hair wa, there's none on it
For the way she pats ma head
has made me bald.
I know she means no harm,
for she'll keep me nice and warm,
On the frosty nichts sae very cauld.

Chorus

It's a dear old land is the Mother land,
and when she sounds the call,
Her boys in her far off other lands
Obey it one and all.
For it is ev'ry Briton's duty,
To do what he can do.
To defend our British Empire,
To stand and see her through.

Chorus

For it's a dear old land,
is the Mother land,
Her sons are ever true.
Her boys in her far off other lands,
Will see her through and through.
It's a dear old home is the homeland,
It's as good as in days of yore.
We are steady aye, and ready,
While the British bull-dog's
watching at the door.

Chorus

It's a peaceful land is the Motherland.
We never want to fight,
But shoulder to shoulder we ever stand,
For everything that's right.
It's a dear old home is the Homeland,
We love her more and more,
We'll fight the German might down
As we've never done before.

Chorus

It's a grand old home is the Homeland,
Then let us pledge that we,
Will all fight for our Motherland,
That Britons shall be free,
That the glory of our Empire,
From us will never fade,
And that we'll defend for ever,
The land our fathers made.

Events of 1916

May–June	Trentino offensive.
31 May	Battle of Jutland.
4 June	The Brusilov offensive.
1 July–18 November	Battle of the Somme.
7 November	Woodrow Wilson re-elected.

OVER THERE

Written by George M. Cohan

Johnnie, get your gun,
Get your gun, get your gun,
Take it on the run,
On the run, on the run.
Hear them calling, you and me,
Every son of liberty.
Hurry right away,
No delay, no delay,
Make your daddy glad
To have had such a lad.
Tell your sweetheart not to pine,
To be proud her boy's in line.

Chorus

Johnnie, get your gun,
Get your gun, get your gun,
Johnnie show the Hun
Who's a son of a gun.
Hoist the flag and let her fly,
Yankee Doodle do or die.
Pack your little kit,
Show your grit, do your bit.
Yankee Doodle fill the ranks,
From the towns and the tanks.
Make your mother proud of you,
And the old Red, White and Blue.

(Chorus – twice)

Over there, over there,
Send the word, send the
word over there –
That the Yanks are coming,
The Yanks are coming,
The drums rum-tumming
Ev'rywhere.
So prepare, say a pray'r,
Send the word, send the word to beware.
We'll be over, we're coming over,
And we won't come back till it's over
Over there.

George M. Cohan

In 1917, America had just entered the war and George M. Cohan composed his greatest hit. Cohan was travelling by train from New Rochelle into New York, when the headlines in the papers being read by everyone on the train gave him inspiration:

"I read those war headlines, and I got to thinking and humming to myself, and for a minute, I thought I was going to dance. I was all finished with both the chorus and the verse by the time I got to town, and I also had a title."

The title was 'Over There'. It had its first public performance by a singer called Charles King in the New Amsterdam theatre at a Red Cross benefit concert.

It was still a time of innocence. The "Doughboys", which is what the American troops were nicknamed, were eager to march to war, but as yet had experienced none of the horrors. Enthusiasm was the order of the day and the success of 'Over There' reflected that, and was a potent weapon for those organising the US Army Recruitment Drive. Cohan's contribution to the war effort was belatedly recognised when he was awarded the Congressional Medal of Honor in 1940. He died in 1942 aged 64.

Many Broadway stars played an active role on the American home front during World War I. Al Jolson and others entertained the troops and tirelessly raised millions in war bond drives. Flo Ziegfeld dressed his *Follies* chorus girls in uniforms for numerous patriotic songs and tableaux.

Anna Held

Very little is known about Anna Held's early life. During her teen years, she went from being a factory girl, living in poverty in London's Whitechapel, to being a much-loved Parisian showgirl.

In the USA, Florenz Ziegfeld Jr was already a rich man; his father owned a successful music business. He saw Held on stage in Paris and fell in love with her. Held moved to the United States and, even though they didn't legally marry, they lived together for a number of years. She became a major hit in the United States when she went on tour with her productions.

All Ziegfeld did was provide the money for Anna's productions. She organised everything else – her costumes, the music and the chorus girls.

She also lectured at various universities about acting, did advertisements for Bebé Jumeau dolls and endorsed products such as corsets, toiletries and cosmetics. Anna had become the world's first, great superstar. Tens upon thousands lined the streets to try to get into her productions. She was described by one reporter as "A pretty girl, with a lovely Roly-Poly figure". By the early 1900s, however, she was starting to wear out. She'd been on constant tour for years. It was she who convinced Ziegfeld to do a show without her, based on the French production of Folies-Bergères. The production did not include a story line, but featured many girls doing vaudeville and music-hall-type acts. They were dubbed the Ziegfeld Follies.

In 1914, World War I broke out, and Anna's beloved France was in ruins. She immediately returned to Paris and began contributing to the war effort. She, and a troupe of willing entertainers, toured hospitals and the front line, entertaining the allied troops. She made them smile and eased their grief as well as working in the Red Cross hospitals. She spent over US$2 million of her own money, obtaining truckloads of medical supplies shipped over from the United States (which, at this time, was not in the war). She opened up her Paris home as a house for Belgian refugees. In 1915, while en-route to an allied military base, where she was to perform, she was captured by the German army, who

didn't believe she was really an entertainer, but a spy. (Mata Hari, an exotic dancer, was executed by the Allied Army during WWI as she was thought to be a spy). She spent ages in a prison camp, before one guard finally convinced his superiors that she was the famous Anna Held. She was released, on the condition that she do a show for the German troops, which she did. Anna continued working in Paris, for the war effort, but her health started to fail her and she returned to the United States. She constantly wrote to the president, begging him to join the war, as the allied troops needed help desperately, but he continued to decline.

Back in New York Anna continued with spectacular productions as well as movies in Hollywood. All of her money went to the allied war effort. Her hard work, however, meant her physical decline. She collapsed on the stage, in 1917, and was diagnosed as having a type of cancer. She died soon after, and never got to see the end of the war. Her funeral was attended by thousands, and almost everyone in show business was there, except for Ziegfeld himself.

Above: Anna Held.

Lieutenant James Reese Europe

James Reese Europe is cited in books about ragtime and early jazz as the most respected black bandleader of the 1910s, but he is also acknowledged among World War I historians because of his musical compositions inspired by wartime experiences and the achievements of his band, known as the 369th US Infantry "Hell Fighters" Band.

Especially remarkable are the songs 'On Patrol In No Man's Land' and 'All Of No Man's Land Is Ours', recorded in March 1919. These songs about the war have an authenticity lacking in other popular recordings of the day. Tin Pan Alley produced hundreds, perhaps thousands, of songs about the war, but popular singers like Henry Burr, Irving Kaufman, Billy Murray and Nora Bayes never fought in the war they sang about.

Jim Europe and his musicians had experienced the war's horrors first-hand and, after the Armistice, had been among the first African-American soldiers to enter a disarmed Germany. They were members of the most famous black unit of the war. When he returned triumphantly in 1919 from the Western Front, Lieutenant Europe had fresh opportunities for playing his music to a wider audience. The Pathé record company secured his services as an exclusive artist and heavily promoted Europe's music.

A number of the recordings give musical form to the military experience of Europe's musicians. The lyrics of 'On Patrol In No Man's Land' describe a small unit attack. In 'All Of No Man's Land Is Ours', a soldier whose ship has docked phones a loved one. Another song evokes a victory parade for returning heroes, the kind in which Europe and his musicians proudly marched. Two songs celebrate a return home.

Europe's group performed as a military band but there was a freedom and swing evident in the band's Pathé recordings that no other military bands attempted. The music is rich in syncopation and jazz effects. Europe's Pathé records are radically different from those he made for the Victor Talking Machine Company five years earlier, right before the war (his last four titles for Victor were recorded on 10 February 1914).

The Pathé company proudly promoted Europe's discs by issuing a special flier announcing new titles: "Eleven records of the world's greatest exponent of syncopation just off the press." In bold type, the flier announced, "Jim Europe's jazz will live forever." Sadly, his music fell into relative obscurity.

43

Above: James Reese Europe and his band.

James Europe was born in 1888 and, when he was nine, his family moved to Washington D.C., where he lived for a time only houses away from John Philip Sousa. He would have known very well the extraordinary excitement Sousa and his famous US Marine Corps Band could generate.

Before the war, Europe had worked closely with the husband-and-wife team Vernon and Irene Castle.

In 1914 he signed a contract with the Castles to tour England, France and other countries, but declaration of war changed those plans. Vernon Castle, born in England, volunteered to serve in the British Aviation Corps. He was to die in a plane accident in Texas on 15 February 1918. Regular public performances by Europe and the Castles ended in 1915.

On 18 September 1916, Europe enlisted in the 15th New York Infantry, a black National Guard regiment formed in Harlem. Noble Sissle, a friend and fellow musician, joined a week later. Pianist Eubie Blake, with slim chances of becoming an officer like Europe and Sissle, took over the administration of Europe's music business – a step which proved invaluable to Europe. Why Europe joined when he did is a little puzzling. War fever played no part. Reid Badger suggests that Europe joined because he believed "a national guard unit in Harlem could become an important organisation of benefit to the entire community". Europe evidently felt his enlistment set a good example for others in

Harlem. Still in New York, Europe passed the officer's exam, was commissioned and about to take command of a machine gun company when his regimental commander, Colonel William Hayward, induced him to organise a military brass band. Money was allocated so Europe could recruit talented musicians. Within the year, Lieutenant Jim Europe and his regiment, recently redesignated the 369th US Infantry, were in France earning a superb reputation for entertaining countless soldiers, officers and French civilians.

Assigned by General Pershing to serve with the French 161st Division, the 369th Infantry was soon training at Givry-en-Argonne. Here Europe learned to fire French machine guns prior to moving into the active trenches. Europe's Regimental Commander later wrote: "... We are proud to think our boys were the first Negro Americans in the trenches. (Lt.) Jim Europe was certainly the first Negro officer in. You can imagine how important he feels!" But senior officers realised that a top-quality band was invaluable for troop morale, so in August 1918 Lieutenant Europe and his musicians were ordered back from the front. Europe then entertained thousands of soldiers in camps and hospitals – an extremely important contribution to the Allied cause.

Europe's combat duties had included going out on patrol, and a harrowing experience inspired the lyrics for 'On Patrol in No Man's Land', which he committed to paper while in a hospital after a gas attack. Sissle later wrote that Europe performed it at the piano while the band made "all the sound effects of a bombardment". The speed with which Europe wrote the song after an actual attack is remarkable, and little time was wasted before it was recorded. Nothing is romanticised. The lyrics give listeners some sense of what being in No Man's Land was like. An officer leads men "over the top" of the trenches for patrol, warns them of danger from German weapons and gives an order to attack. Newspapers reported what was happening to soldiers overseas, but here the experience of battle is conveyed in artistic form – in Europe's case, in ragtime. Nothing in American popular song at that time was quite like this.. All of Europe's musicians participate in recreating the chaos of battle. A companion piece is 'All Of No Man's Land Is Ours', sung by Noble Sissle. Although the title expresses the pride of victorious soldiers, this is really a love song. A soldier has docked and phones a sweetheart to announce his arrival home, his intentions to marry her and even his plans for children ("Just think how happy we will be – I mean we three").

After the returning soldiers phoned family, friends and sweethearts – that is, anyone not already at the pier greeting the ships – the men proceeded to their next destination for demobilisation. Europe's men arrived in New York in February, 1919, and this song by Sissle and Europe was probably composed shortly after that homecoming. It was recorded one month later.

'How 'ya Gonna Keep 'em Down On The Farm?', recorded in March of 1919, is also vocalised by Noble Sissle. This song became incredibly popular when introduced in early 1919. Many recorded it, with versions by Nora Bayes and Arthur Fields especially popular. The song's lyrics question if American men returning from battlefields and especially from "Paree" will readily settle down to the chores of farm life. Big-city lights and jazz clubs will be far more alluring.

The song arguably took on a political significance when African-Americans performed it. How would America keep returning black soldiers "down" after they had tasted equality while serving in France? Jim Europe's musicians were not the only blacks to record this at the time. Ford Dabney's band recorded it weeks after Europe's did.

Europe suffered a fatal stabbing two days after his band recorded six titles for Pathé. That recording session took place on 7 May 1919. There was no clear motive for the stabbing. Accounts differ, but it seems that backstage during a Boston concert Europe reprimanded Herbert Wright for the drummer's unprofessional habit of walking on and off stage while other acts performed. When Europe ordered Herbert Wright to leave Europe's dressing room, the unstable drummer produced a pen knife and stabbed the bandleader in the neck. Europe was rushed to City Hospital, where he soon died.

Europe could have contributed significantly to popular music in the 1920s and beyond. He was ambitious, talented and energetic. New opportunities presented themselves in 1919 and Jim Europe's best days may have been ahead. Unfortunately we will never know what his contribution might have been.

The Cinema

The early part of the 20th century was the era of the silent movie, although an orchestra or pianist would accompany the film, sat in front of the screen or in a "pit". Most films were imported from the USA as they were more advanced in terms of technique and narrative than in Britain. Comedies directly involving the war were avoided and, because of America's neutral stance for most of the war, most films were produced primarily for a civilian audience. Shows were sectioned into short films of 10–15 minutes, news bulletins and very basic cartoons such as the Kineto war maps which were pioneered at this time. It was difficult to stage film performances at the front line but wartime cinemas could be located either in the small towns behind the lines that had escaped shelling or in permanent bases. The Bull Ring training ground at Etaples had its own cinema which was extremely popular.

ALL OF NO MAN'S LAND IS OURS

James Reese Europe

Hello, Central,
Hello, hurry,
Give me four-oh-three;
Hello, Mary,
Hello, Jerry,
Yes, yes, this is me!
Just landed at the pier
And found the telephone.
We've been parted for a year,
Thank God, at last I'm home!
Haven't time to talk a lot,
Though I'm feeling mighty gay;
Listen, sweet forget-me-not,
I've only time to say:
All of No Man's Land is ours, dear,
Now I have come back home to you,
My honey true.
Wedding bells in Junie-June
All will tell by the tunie-tune,
The victory's won, the war is over,
The whole wide world is
wreathed in clover!
Then, hand-in-hand we'll stroll
through life, dear.
Just think how happy we will be,
I mean, we three.
We'll pick a bungalow among the
fragrant boughs,
And spend our honeymoon
with the blooming flowers.
All of No Man's Land is ours.

46

Above: Soldiers at the front in World War I.

Cinema was enjoyed by all classes of people. Owing to the limited amount of comedy available, the action of going to the cinema seems to have been primarily a social one. The troops were uninterested in the newsreels and it seems that the film programmes consisted exclusively of repeat comedy and little more. Soldiers wanted to see films to escape from reality; hence the emphasis on farce and humour that was the dominant theme of all cinemas at the front. Although comedies stayed resolutely away from the subject of the war, focusing on home front concerns that the troops would have found patronising and irrelevant, cinema was still the greatest form of escapism and, as it was still a relatively new invention, it is easy to see why the soldiers appreciated it so much.

War comedies were scarce, but some were still produced. It seems that these were preferred at the front to the more staple forms of melodrama, and were often repeated extensively. Many cinema programmes at the front placed great emphasis on the fact that their shows changed weekly, even though there was limited choice. Farces ridiculing the Germans, especially those with a "very fat Kaiser", were the major theme. Leading this genre were the comedies from the Keystone studio and Harold Lloyd, although again the war as a direct topic was infrequent and the Germans appeared as background characters. Films stuck to clichéd formulae of melodrama or gross comedy. However, as these comedies were produced for the home front, they placed a heavy emphasis on army promotion and recruitment. Increasing morale was a key theme that was often unsubtle and was not always appreciated. The main military character was never shown as anything other than brave or noble, the comedy itself taking second place to the central theme of morality. One of these farces, *The Submarine Pirate* (1918, Keystone), was so successful in this respect that it was used by the navy to help recruitment.

The best comedies of the war were, of course, the most subversive. Charlie Chaplin was already established as a leading star of the silent screen and he continued to produce films during the war that were seen in a far better light than the more irrelevant melodramas. However, although he supported the war cause, Chaplin did not fight and there was considerable animosity from the troops towards him as they claimed he was producing films on a subject about which he knew nothing. As an American citizen, Chaplin did not have to fight, but his continued public drive for war bonds made him the focus of critical ire with several trench songs featuring him:

Above: Charlie Chaplin became the subject of many trench songs.

CHARLIE CHAPLIN

The Moon shines Bright
on Charlie Chaplin.
His boots are cracking,
for want of blacking,
And his khaki trousers
they want mending,
Before we send him,
To the Dardanelles.

And a slightly less vehement version:

They say as Charlie Chaplin ain't
A doing of his bit
Yet all the same with all the boys
He sure has made a hit;
He licks the Western Cowboy and
His Bronco-busting trick –
Of all the reels upon the film
Old Charlie is the pick.

During the war years some of the films that were shown, both at home and on the Western front, were:

1914 The Battle at Elderbush Gulch, Cabiria, Gertie the Dinosaur, Home Sweet Home, In the Land of the War Canoes: A Drama of Kwakiutl Indian Life on the Northwest Coast, Judith of Bethulia, Mabel's Married Life, The Patchwork Girl of Oz, The Perils of Pauline, Tillie's Punctured Romance, Uncle Tom's Cabin.

1915 Alias Jimmy Valentine, The Birth of a Nation, Carmen, The Cheat, Ghosts, Hypocrites, A Tale of Two Cities.

1916 Eleanor's Catch, The Floorwalker, Intolerance, The Ocean Waif, The Pawnshop, The Rink, Les Vampires.

1917 The Immigrant, Joan the Woman, The Outlaw and His Wife, Teddy at the Throttle, Thomas Graal's Best Child.

1918 Amarilly of Clothes-line Alley, Hearts of the World, The Kid, Stella Maris, The Whispering Chorus.

Despite some of the more negative songs about him, Chaplin remained extremely popular. His performance relied more on slapstick than melodrama, giving a greater degree of escapism than farces concerning morality and home. Chaplin was appreciated by a wide audience – it was a communal activity going to one of his films, and knowing there would be others present laughing at his antics. Lastly, Chaplin's comedy may have been crude, but at the time it was still novel. Farce and slapstick made a welcome break from the intense dramatics of the silent screen.

During 1917 the theatres and music halls in London were putting on the following shows:

Title	Venue
Airs & Graces	Palace
Any Old Thing	Pavilion
Arlette	Shaftesbury
The Beauty Spot	Gaiety
The Better 'Ole	Oxford
The Bing Girls Are There	Oxford
	Alhambra
The Boy	Adelphi
Bubbly	Comedy
Carminetta	Prince of Wales
Cash on Delivery	Prince of Wales
Cheep	Vaudeville
Hanky Panky	Empire
Here and There	Empire
Pamela	Palace
Round the Map	Alhambra
Smile	Garrick
Suzette	Globe
Topsy Turvy	Empire
Yes, Uncle!	Prince of Wales
Zig-Zag	Hippodrome

This rousing song was written in 1898 and was first sung in the Boer War.

GOODBYE, DOLLY

Written by Will D. Cobb and Paul Barnes

Goodbye, Dolly, I must leave you
Though it breaks my heart to go.
Something tells me I am needed
At the Front to fight the foe.
See the soldiers boys are marching
And I can no longer stay.
Hark I hear the bugle calling
Goodbye, Dolly Gray.

Wipers was the soldiers' name for the town of Ypres, although the soldiers singing it would have substituted the name of the town nearest to their posting. Despite the starkness of the message, this is an ironic sentimental song to the tune of a ballad called 'Sing Me To Sleep'.

FAR, FAR FROM WIPERS

Far, far from Wipers I long to be.
Where German snipers can't get at me.
Dark is my dugout, cold are my feet.
Waiting for Whizzbangs
to send me to sleep.

Events of 1917

22 January	"Peace without Victory" speech by Woodrow Wilson.
1 February	Unrestricted submarine warfare declared by Germany, again.
24 February	The sinking of the *Laconia*.
15 March	Tsar Nicholas abdicates.
March–September	Russia collapses.
2 April	Woodrow Wilson asks the House of Representatives to declare war on Germany.
6 April	United States declares war on Germany, thus entering World War I.
16–29 April	Chemin des Dames offensive.
April	Battles of Arras and Vimy Ridge.
April	Nivelle offensive.
June	Battle of Messines.
6 July	Aquaba captured by Arabs led by T. E.Lawrence.
16 July–10 November	Third Battle of Ypres.
6 August	Aleksander Fyodorovich Kerensky appointed prime minister of Russia.
October	Battle of Caporetto.
7 November	Kerensky's government overthrown by Bolsheviks.
10 November	British reach Passchendaele.
November	Battle of Cambrai.
3 December	German-Russian armistice.
9 December	Jerusalem captured by the British.

FRED KARNO'S ARMY

We are Fred Karno's army, the ragtime infantry.
We cannot fight, we cannot shoot, what bleedin' use are we?
And when we get to Berlin we'll hear the Kaiser say,
"Hoch, hoch! Mein Gott, what a bloody
fine lot, are the ragtime infantry."

Fred Karno's Army

Fred Karno was a popular American entertainer who toured the USA, and his name became one of the nicknames that were given to the American troops by the British Tommies.

Comedy was essential to provide the troops with ways to cope with the situation at the front, and maintaining morale was vital to keep them fighting. In the context of the Great War, humour and morale become intertwined, one re-inforcing the other.

Although the comedy of World War I was often exclusive and insular, and therefore symptomatic of rebellion, it was a useful way of binding groups of people together to help them overcome situations which they possibly would not have been able to face otherwise. The troops were in a situation in which they needed to find common ground quickly, and one of their natural instincts was to do this through humour. They were cut adrift from their pre-war lives and needed to form social groups with which they could relate. The nature of the war meant that as a community they were segregated from the conventional behaviour patterns of the home front, and they therefore created cultural signifiers specific to their own situation. Humour helped to bridge this culture shock.

OH, IT'S A LOVELY WAR!

Written by J. P. Long and Maurice Scott

Up to your waist in water, up to your eyes in slush,
Using the kind of language that makes the sergeant blush,
Who wouldn't join the army? That's what we all enquire.
Don't we pity the poor civilian sitting by the fire.

(Chorus)

Oh, oh, oh it's a lovely war.
Who wouldn't be a soldier, eh? Oh it's a shame to take the pay.
As soon as reveille has gone we feel just as heavy as lead,
But we never get up till the sergeant brings our breakfast up to bed.
Oh, oh, oh, it's a lovely war.

What do we want with eggs and ham when we've got plum and apple jam?
Form fours. Right turn. How shall we spend the money we earn?
Oh, oh, oh it's a lovely war.
When does a soldier grumble? When does he make a fuss?
No one is more contented in all the world than us.
Oh it's a cushy life, boys, really we love it so:
Once a fellow was sent on leave and simply refused to go.

(Chorus)

Often the troops used "gallows" humour to alleviate their stress. Civilians who had never fought in the trenches could find some of the soldiers' humour shocking and offensive at times with their seeming irreverence. Although they did not laugh at the loss of comrades the troops did use comedy to express their relief at still being alive. Indeed, many a time the troops laughed at the experience of death and the extreme conditions they were living in. 'Oh, What A Lovely War' was written in 1917 by J. P. Long and Maurice Scott as a music-hall tune and adapted by the soldiers.

War Records

The outbreak of World War I both stimulated and disrupted the development of the gramophone. The Gramophone Company at Hayes in England was partly given over to war production while demand grew for portable gramophones at the frontline. Songs like 'It's a Long, Long Way to Tipperary' and 'Till The Boys Come Home' proved popular at the front, and have come to epitomise those years for successive generations.

The new technology was used to capture the sounds of the war. The Gramophone Company recorded the roar of the big guns on the frontline at Lille. Following the Armistice, the Company recorded the ceremony that accompanied the burial of the the Unknown Soldier at Westminster Abbey. It was the first ever sound recording of a major public event.

During 1918 the theatres and music halls in London were putting on the following shows:

Title	Venue
As You Were	Pavilion
The Bing Boys on Broadway	Alhambra
Box 'O Tricks	Hippodrome
Buzz Buzz	Vaudeville
Flora	Prince of Wales
Going Up	Gaiety
Hullo, America!	Palace

W

*Jack Dunn, son of a gun, over in
France today,
Keeps fit doing his bit up to
his eyes in clay.
Each night after a fight to
pass the time along,
He's got a little gramophone
that plays this song:*

*Take me back to dear old Blighty!
Put me on the train for London town!
Take me over there,
Drop me ANYWHERE,
Liverpool, Leeds, or Birmingham,
well, I don't care!
I should love to see my best girl,
Cuddling up again we soon should be,
WHOA!!!
Tiddley iddley ighty,
Hurry me home to Blighty,
Blighty is the place for me!*

*Bill Spry, started to fly,
up in an aeroplane,
In France, taking a chance,
wish'd he was down again.
Poor Bill, feeling so ill,
yell'd out to Pilot Brown:
"Steady a bit, yer fool! we're turning
upside down!"*

TAKE ME BACK TO DEAR OLD BLIGHTY

composed by A. J. Mills, Fred Godfrey and Bennett Scott

Take me back to dear old Blighty!
Put me on the train for London town!
Take me over there,
Drop me ANYWHERE,
Liverpool, Leeds, or Birmingham,
well, I don't care!
I should love to see my best girl,
Cuddling up again we soon should be,
WHOA!!!
Tiddley iddley ighty,
Hurry me home to Blighty,
Blighty is the place for me!

Jack Lee, having his tea,
says to his pal MacFayne,
"Look, chum, apple and plum! It's
apple and plum again!
Same stuff, isn't it rough?
Fed up with it I am!
Oh! for a pot of Aunt Eliza's
raspb'ry jam!

Take me back to dear old Blighty!
Put me on the train for London town!
Take me over there,
Drop me ANYWHERE,
Liverpool, Leeds, or Birmingham,
well, I don't care!
I should love to see my best girl,
Cuddling up again we soon should be,

WHOA!!!
Tiddley iddley ighty,
Hurry me home to Blighty,
Blighty is the place for me!

One day Mickey O'Shea stood
in a trench somewhere,
So brave, having a shave,
and trying to part his hair.
Mick yells, dodging the shells and
lumps of dynamite:
"Talk of the Crystal Palace on a
firework night!"

Take me back to dear old Blighty!
Put me on the train for London town!
Take me over there,
Drop me ANYWHERE,
Liverpool, Leeds, or Birmingham,
well, I don't care!
I should love to see my best girl,
Cuddling up again we soon should be,
WHOA!!!
Tiddley iddley ighty,
Hurry me home to Blighty,
Blighty is the place for me!

Events of 1918

8 January	President Wilson delivers his 14-point speech to the Congress.
3 March	Treaty of Brest-Litovsk signed by Soviet Russia and the Central Powers of Germany, Austria-Hungary and Turkey.
15 March	Soviets ratify the Brest-Litovsk Treaty.
March–June	Ludendorff offensive.
April	Zeebruggge Raid.
16 May	Espionage Act.
June–July	Piave offensive.
16–17 July	Bolsheviks murder Tsar Nicholas and his family.
17 July	Archangel expedition.
29 September	Allies break through the Hindenberg Line.
September–October	Battle of Megiddo.
September	St Mihiel offensive.
September–November	Battle of Meuse-Argonne.
28 October	German sailors mutiny.
5 November	Allies accept the 14 points of peace.
9 November	Kaiser Wilhelm abdicates.
10 November	German republic founded.
11 November	World War I ends. Central Powers are forced to annul the Brest-Litovsk Treaty.

TILL WE MEET AGAIN

Written by Jack Judge and Harry Williams

There's a song in the land of the lily,
Each sweetheart has heard with a sigh.
Over high garden walls this sweet
echo falls
As a soldier boy whispers goodbye:
Smile the while you kiss me sad adieu
When the clouds roll by I'll come to you.
Then the skies will seem more blue,
Down in Lover's Lane, my dearie.
Wedding bells will ring so merrily
Every tear will be a memory.
So wait and pray each night for me
Till we meet again.
Tho' goodbye means the birth
of a tear drop,
Hello means the birth of a smile.
And the smile will erase the tear
blighting trace,
When we meet in the after awhile.
Smile the while you kiss me sad adieu
When the clouds roll by I'll come to you.
Then the skies will seem more blue
Down in Lover's Lane, my dearie,
Wedding bells will ring so merrily
Every tear will be a memory.
So wait and pray each night for me
Till we meet again.

57 *Above: A kiss goodbye for a loved one off to war.*

In Flanders Fields

'In Flanders Fields' remains to this day one of the most memorable war poems ever written. It is a lasting legacy of the terrible battle in Ypres during the spring of 1915. Here is the story of the making of that poem.

Major John McCrae had been a doctor for years, after graduating from the University of Toronto. He had served as a surgeon in the South African War in the dressing stations but even that did not prepare him for what he witnessed in World War I. He was attached to the 1st Field Artillery Brigade, and spent 17 days treating injured men of all nations, Canadians, British, Indians, French and Germans, in Ypres. McCrae later wrote of it: "I wish I could embody on paper some of the varied sensations of that 17 days ... 17 days of Hades! At the end of the first day if anyone had told us we had to spend 17 days there, we would have folded our hands and said it could not have been done."

It was one death in particular, that of a young friend and former student, Lieutenant Alexis Helmer who had been killed by a shell burst on 2 May 1915 which inspired him to write a poem. Helmer had been buried that day in the little cemetery outside McCrae's dressing station, and, in the absence of a chaplain, McCrae had performed the funeral ceremony.

On 3 May McCrae, already the author of several medical texts, sat in the cemetery and saw the wild poppies in the ditches all about. Cyril Allinson, a 22-year-old sergeant-major, was delivering mail when he noticed McCrae. The major looked up as Allinson approached, but continued writing. Allinson observed quietly. "His face was very tired but calm as he wrote," Allinson recollected. "He looked around from time to time, his eyes straying to Helmer's grave."

Five minutes later McCrae had finished, he took his mail from Allinson and, without saying a word, handed his notepad to Allinson who was moved by what he read: "The poem was exactly an exact description of the scene in front of us both. He used the word blow in that line because the poppies actually were being blown that morning by a gentle east wind. It never occurred to me at that time that it would ever be published. It seemed to me just an exact description of the scene."

In fact, the poem was very nearly not published. Dissatisfied with it, McCrae tossed it away, but a fellow officer retrieved it and sent it to newspapers in England where it was published in *Punch* on 8 December 1915.

IN FLANDERS FIELDS

Written by John McCrae

*In Flanders fields the poppies blow
Between the crosses, row on row,
That mark our place; and in the sky
The larks, still bravely singing, fly
Scarce heard amid the guns below.
We are the Dead. Short days ago
We lived, felt dawn, saw sunset glow,
Loved and were loved, and now we lie
In Flanders fields.
Take up our quarrel with the foe:
To you from failing hands we throw
The torch; be yours to hold it high.
If ye break faith with us who die
We shall not sleep, though poppies grow
In Flanders fields.*

World War I ("The Great War") was fought from 1914-1918. There were 8.6 million casualties, with the Allied Powers (the victors) losing 5.1 million and the Central Powers losing 3.5 million. The war was devastating to all the countries involved, and was known as the "war to end all wars" – until World War II began.

59

Above: The poppy became the symbol of remembrance of both World Wars.

Interlude

The Bugle

The word "bugle", first recorded in middle-English (roughly 1200–1500), was adopted from an old French word derived from the Latin *buculus* or ox (diminutive of *bos* or young bull), and is thus an abbreviation of the earlier term bugle horn. Contemporary terms include (French) *clairon* and (German) *Signalhorn*. Modern bugles of copper or brass used by the armed forces of most countries and by British, civilian youth bands have a compact, twice-wound form with a small bell, which was authorised in 1858. This or the once-wound bugle horn was first used by German Jäger units in the Seven Years War. The English Light Dragoons adopted them in 1764 and the Grenadier Guards in 1772.

British calls usually comprise a "battalion" call, to identify the unit required to obey the call, followed by the "duty" involved; along with company calls. Drummers had beaten tactical direction to battalions, certainly from the mid-1500s, well before we believe that marching in step occurred beyond the parade ground. However, in the 16th and 17th centuries, drum signalling to British troops was so significant that both England and Scotland had their respective English and Scottish marches. The first English march was believed to be for drum alone and was so important that, circa 1631, King Charles I felt it necessary to ordain that the English march for rallying troops in battle be taught once more throughout the realm.

The war for independence in America saw a need for more lightly equipped troops than the sturdily mannered infantry of the day to combat the enemy's skirmishing way of operation. This also applied later in the Peninsular War in Spain. The 5th Battalion, 60th Rifles, commanded by Lieutenant Colonel Baron de Rottenburg was the first British unit to take tactical direction from bugle horns.

The Bugle Calls

Rouse "Come, make a move and show a leg – Why dilly dally? Now, don't you hear? Get out of bed, it's past Reveille! Get out now, sharp, for the day's begun". Sometimes called "The Donkey", the Rouse was to awaken troops and, 15 minutes later, was followed by the reveille call, when troops turned out.

Reveille A call more popular for its attractive sound than its requirement!

Meal Calls On the first meal call, "Oh! Come to the cookhouse door, boys, Come to the cookhouse door", the Orderly Men from each barrack room reported to the cookhouse to draw the rations, supervised by the Orderly Officer and assorted Orderly Sergeants. At the second call, "Oh pick 'em up, pick 'em up hot potatoes oh, pick 'em up, pick 'em up hot potatoes oh!", troops began their meal, visited by the battalion duty officer etc. The doggerel words to Payne's march 'Punjab', "Why should I draw rations when I'm not the Orderly Man" are from this.

Everything's done on the run
... Listen! There hark!
Same old remark, heard in
the Ark, 'Half an hour for,
warning for p'rade".
 Or:
"Just a half an hour they
give us all to dress, lots of
time to turn out afresh!
Things will be bad if
you're not there just the
same ... the Ord'ly
Sergeant, he'll jot down
your name.
Then take my tip boys,
half an hour you've
got. Just look sharp
and get on the spot!"

Quarter "Quarter my
boys! Time to make a
move". Reactions to
these were dependent
upon the parade to
which troops were
bidden. If a
company parade,
the troops mustered in time for
the parade to be handed over at the time
shown in Company Detail but for a
battalion parade companies were formed up
in time for the Quarter Call. Then they
could march on to the markers when the
Advance was sounded; (i.e. not the Fall In,
as the companies had already "fallen in").
With no call for markers, i.e. the right-hand
men of companies, Orderly Corporals were

Half Hour and Quarter Hour Calls
Half "Warning for parade! It's half an hour
they give us to get in good trim, Half an
hour before those bugles call 'Fall in'.
Lor! There's a lot to be done – shave, wash
and clean the old gun!

61 *Above: Irving Berlin's comical World War I song.*

used in some regiments. In many cases, individual battalions had their own, specific form-up procedure comprising that personal blend of drum, flute, pipe calls and verbal orders assimilated over hundreds of years.

Fall In "That's the call for us all. Fall in now the short and the tall! In you fall great and small, see you stand up smart at the call!" or "Fall in 'A', fall in 'B', fall in all the companies" ('A' and 'B' means 'A' Company etc).

Dismiss, or No Parade "Oh, there's no parade today, Oh, there's no parade today, It's jolly seldom that we get the chance to stay away". It was a final call indicating in some regiments that there was no more work so men could go home or at other times that a particular parade was over or was cancelled.

Post Call "Letters from Lousy Lou boys, letters from Lousy Lou" or "Maybe there's one for me boys, maybe there's one for you"; or the slightly purified, "There goes the call for letters, latest from 'home sweet home'". A call at which Orderly (In Waiting) Corporals collected the mail from the post room for distribution.

Fatigue Call "I called them; I called them, they wouldn't come. I called them; I called them, they wouldn't come at all!". Sounded routinely for men under this punishment to assemble for detail, or, in the working day, for those men detailed to do fatigues from the Duty Company.

Orderly Sergeants "The orderly sergeants are wanted now – orderly sergeants to run! Come". To summon Company Orderly Sergeants/Sergeants in Waiting, it could be sounded at any time but always for RSM's Detail (about mid-morning). Orderly Corporals was also used as a matter of routine, CQMS rarely but if CSM were blown for, serious matters were afoot. (For these others: "Now, 'Flags', come answer your call, I say, 'Flags', come answer your call; Come! Come!" for CSM and CQMS and, "Oh! Ord'ly corporals has gone again. Raise your elbows and run!" for the Orderly Corporals.

Parade for Guard A call with an obvious function, which was preceded by the Half Hour and Quarter calls.

Guard Salute Sounded in succession by the Drummers of the Old and New Guards when presenting arms to each other as a part of the relief procedure.

Orderly Room "Now it's all Non-coms who are on duty and officers answer the call! Colonel's in his chair – you bet he won't spare any prisoners at all. 'Tis orderly room!" Usually timed for just before lunch to interfere as little as possible with training, this called for Commanding Officers' Orders (/Memoranda) where summary justice was dispensed and commanding officer's interviews given.

Orders "Come for orders, come for orders, now be sharp, hurry up! Come for orders; you know the Corps is waiting for the orders of the day – So come, let 'em have the news!" Usually sounded when daily orders were complete and ready for collection by company clerks or company runners and thus often blown in the afternoon.

Officers' Call "Officers, come when you're called! Adjutant's shouted and bawled! Colonel he'll swear that you crawled! Come! Come! Come!" A call rarely heard and thus almost unknown in some regiments, the Brigade of Guards has it as an essential part of their various battalion "form-ups" (a subject worthy of separate study).

Pioneers Call "Pioneer, pioneer, pioneer there's a dog been on the square! Pioneer, pioneer, pioneer and it's left its business there!" – A rare call as the Quartermaster guarded his tradesmen jealously. Battalion pioneers were "in-house" tradesmen rather than members of the Royal Pioneer Corps (now Royal Logistic Corps) and particularly provided tree-felling and explosives expertise. An alternative set of words is: "Come along, Pioneer, you are wanted here, to try and clear the way! Look alive, Pioneer! You must work, no fear, or we'll be here all day!"

Band/Drummers/Signallers Calls "It's time we heard the band – they haven't played all day" or "Now let the band strike up, and play us home today." And "Drummers all, big and small, don't you hear the Drummers Call?" The Adjutant might decide to devote the first 20 minutes of parade to foot and arms drill at the halt and then use Band or Drummers call when it was time to begin marching. Further, although the Drums were the signallers until the end of the 19th century, as their functions broadened the need for a more specific call can be understood. Hence "Signallers, come!"

School Call "Now go to school and learn to write, It gets you on … for the stripe". Usually sounded during the morning when the day's education began.

Rations "Go for the rations Ord'ly

man, stale bread and meat and plenty of bone". It signalled the bulk issue of rations to messes and cookhouses from the rations store, was usually sounded around mid-day and was an event attended by the Orderly/Picquet Officer, Sergeant and Corporal. Young officers were taught to examine meat by touch and smell because checking its fitness for consumption was central to this part of their duty.

Fire Call "There's a fire, there's a fire, there's a fire". Sounded by the first Drummer to spot a fire or, at last, by the Guard Drummer, it was always followed by the Double, was taken up by all Drummers and was answered at the double. As the Guard Drummer had to navigate his route swiftly sounding this call, by the 1960s he frequently used the battalion bicycle. It was invariably followed by the Double. When taught with the Double, the words sometimes were, "There's a fire, there's a fire, there's a fire. Run and get the engine boys and put the beggar out". The engine in this case was the Fire Picquet's cart, which contained fire apparatus of the period.

Double "Run you buggers, run you buggers, run you buggers, run". This could follow any call and invariably meant trouble, either from an alarm or for those summoned by the call preceding.

General Salute A call sounded by the Guard Drummer when the Quarter Guard paid compliments to the commanders of formations in which the battalion was serving. Other brigadiers and generals would be offered compliments but without a General Salute.

Parade for Picquet The Picquet, sometimes called the Reinforcement Guard was mounted at Retreat and could be used in emergencies, whilst the Quarter Guard was in the Guardroom area to protect the safe, property and detained prisoners until ordered otherwise. Otherwise, the Picquet provided emergency fire cover.

Retreat This call has always signalled the change from day to night routine and is summarised as, "the end of the soldier's working day, except for duties and punishment". There is no evidence that it or retreat marches or drum beatings have ever meant anything else. This change to night routine meant the Picquet was mounted, stores and armouries had been locked and the Quarter Guard turned out for inspection by the Guard Commander. Later this was also the time to mount the new Barrack Guard. The unit flag was lowered (normally by the Guard Drummer, once he had completed sounding Retreat). The Evening Gun would also be fired at this stage.

Tattoo Comprising the First Post and the Last Post it is thought to derive from the system of closing town gates wherein once sentries were posted. The Picquet Officer accompanied by the Picquet Serjeant would inspect all sentry posts, with a call being blown to note the first and last sentry posts visited. More recently, the First Post was sounded at 9.30 p.m. signalling the Company Orderly Sergeants to tour barrack rooms, checking nominal rolls en route, at the same time as the Quarter Guard turned out for a Guard Commander's inspection. The Drums then beat a Tattoo sequence on the square ending with the National Anthem followed by the Last Post. At 9.55 p.m. all those on duty, plus the Defaulters, paraded at the Guardroom for inspection. There, the duty non-commissioned officers made their final reports of the day to the Orderly Officer or the Captain of the Week (depending on which of them took this last parade). Until 1914, it was customary for the Drums to beat Retreat or Tattoo on alternate days of the week. The word "tattoo" is believed to have come from the expression "Doe den taptoe" or close the taps – bungs were hammered into barrels and marked with a chalk cross as a simple "closing" expedient, when campaigning in the Low Countries. Germany's *Zapfenstreich* is similar. The Last Post has become a feature of military funerals to signal that service folk are going to their "last posting".

The Field Calls These were modified in their early life by raising them on the stave, in an effort to make them resonate more effectively through battlefield noise. Barrack Calls were also similarly modified but returned to normal in this century.

Lights Out Sounded between 10.15 p.m. and 11 p.m. dependent on battalion custom, this call ordered just what its name says – all lights other than those for personnel on duty to be extinguished and there to be no noise or talking before Reveille.

World War II
1939-1945

Three factors led to the start of World War II. On 28 June 1919 the Treaty of Versailles which drew up the terms and conditions of the peace was signed by Germany and the Allies at the Palace of Versailles, Paris. It was a treaty dictated by the victors and Germany played no part in the negotiations. Under threat of a naval blockade Germany was forced to sign this "diktat". The terms of the treaty were severe and vengeful rather then conciliatory and peaceful, placing military, territorial and financial limitations on Germany.

The second major cause of World War II was an economic one. The collapse of the German economy in the early 1920s and the financial crises which followed the Wall Street Crash of 1929 led to a global period of instability.

The third and final factor was the growth of extreme militant and nationalistic movements. These were often violent and always totalitarian and did not allow for debate or compromise but appealed to fervent patriotism amongst many European people.

One man turned all of these factors to his advantage in his lust for power.

Above: The Treaty of Versailles.

Above: Adolf Hitler.

Workers' Playtime

Workers' Playtime started out on the BBC Home Service and was broadcast live from a factory canteen "somewhere in Britain" with the Ministry of Labour choosing which factory canteens the show would visit.

Throughout the war, Ernest Bevin, the Minister of Labour and National Service, would make an occasional appearance on the shows to congratulate the workers and exhort them to greater efforts. It proved very successful and after the war was over the Government used *Workers' Playtime* to continue to raise the morale of workers, through the rebuilding of Britain and the recovery of the economy.

The BBC were very happy to continue with a show which had proved a national success even if it did mean transporting crew, cable, microphones, two pianos, a producer, two pianists and a bunch of variety artists up and down the country three times a week. On 1 October 1957 the show switched to the Light Programme, a move which seemed to recognise that the programme no longer fostered the national sense of purpose which made it so essential during the war and immediate post-war years. For all 23 years of its existence, the producer was Bill Gates and he would always finish each programme by saying "Good Luck All Workers!". The programme stopped in 1964.

Many famous variety, vocal and comedy artists appeared on the programme over the years such as Arthur Askey, Charlie Chester, Peter Sellers, Tony Hancock, Frankie Howerd, Anne Shelton, Betty Driver, Eve Boswell, Dorothy Squires, Julie Andrews, Eric Morecambe and Ernie Wise, Peter Cavanagh, Janet Brown, Bob Monkhouse, Peter Goodwright, Percy Edwards, Ken Dodd, Ken Platt, Elsie and Doris Waters.

One of the hit songs on the programme was Noel Gay's 'Let the People Sing', which all the factory girls would sing along to at the end of each show.

LET THE PEOPLE SING

Let the people sing.
Let the welcome ring
Anything to kill the blues.
Find a merry song to cheer them
When things all go wrong.

You will find a song
Welcome as a breath of spring.
Therefore, let the people sing.

71

Above: The BBC initially responded to the war
effort by specifically aiming their programming at
civilians engaged in war work.

Later on in the war the BBC broadcast another programme called *Works Wonders* specifically directed at factory workers but allowing the workers themselves to be the stars of the show. Other radio programmes were *Sincerely Yours* featuring Vera Lynn, *Calling Malta* and *Introducing Ann* featuring Anne Shelton, *Hi Gang* with Americans Ben Lyon and Bebe Daniels, *Garrison Theatre* with Jack Warner and *Bandwagon* with Arthur Askey and Richard Murdoch.

Request programmes also featured strongly – for example, *Sandy Calling* with Sandy Macpherson. By 1942 there were more than 50 request programmes on the air. The BBC's output during the war years was not limited to the home front. They broadcast light entertainment to the troops, 12 hours a day, seven days a week. However, one of the most popular programmes during the war, and indeed after it, was called *ITMA*.

ITMA

It's That Man Again! and its catchy signature tune became a war-time institution. The show was named after a topical catchphrase associated with Hitler.

Above: Vera Lynn featured in the radio programme 'Sincerely Yours'.

Whenever he made some new territorial claim, the newspaper headlines would proclaim 'It's That Man Again', and caricature him as short of stature with a silly moustache. Although this title looked fine in print it was a bit of a mouthful to say over the microphone. Something snappier was needed and, since at the beginning of the war everyone seemed acronym crazy (the R.A.F., the A.R.P., E.N.S.A), the programme title was shortened to *ITMA*.

In 1938 the BBC decided that they should have a regular weekly comedy show, similar to the George Burns and Gracie Allen Show which was very popular in the United States. A trial series of four fortnightly shows began on 12 July 1939. The setting was a pirate commercial radio ship, from which Tommy Handley, the renowned Liverpudlian comedian, sent his choice of programmes. He was assisted by Cecilia Eddy as his secretary Cilly, Eric Egan as a mad Russian inventor, Sam Heppner and Lionel Gamlin. The early editions broadcast from London and were modelled on the ground-breaking show *Bandwagon*. However, they were unsuccessful and the show was due to be axed until Hitler himself saved it.

The outbreak of war shook up the BBC schedules and ITMA returned on 19 September 1939 for a weekly series of 21 episodes. These were transmitted from Bristol, where the BBC Variety Department had taken up residence, hoping to avoid the heavy bombing raids expected in London. Every Tuesday night people would tune in to forget their problems as Tommy Handley and his team turned the war and the enemy into a huge joke. In occupied countries people risked imprisonment or death by switching on their secret radio sets just to listen to and laugh at ITMA.

A pirate radio ship was not considered to be a suitable setting during wartime, so a new scenario was sought. In the early days of the war, new government ministries sprang up, almost overnight. It was decided that for the second series Tommy Handley should be "Minister of

Aggravation and Mysteries" at the Office of Twerps. A brand new supporting cast was enlisted, and in the second episode Funf was created, the elusive German spy whose catchphrase "This is Funf speaking" was to work its way into many private telephone conversations over the next few years.

It all helped to make the German propaganda machine seem little more than a wireless joke. One of the regular features in this series was Radio Fakenburg, a take-off of Radio Luxembourg which had stopped broadcasting for the duration. ITMA's increased popularity led to a couple of stage shows which made brief tours. Unfortunately they folded when the Blitz destroyed many of the theatres. Bristol was bombed and so the BBC Variety Department moved to Bangor in North Wales. With escalating bad news for the allies abroad, send-ups of government departments no longer seemed acceptable. Instead, it was felt that ITMA should provide an escape for a war-weary public.

The show was renamed *It's That Sand Again* and began a six-week summer season on 20 June 1941. It was set in a seedy seaside resort called Foaming at the Mouth, with Tommy Handley as the town's mayor. Several soon-to-be-famous characters were launched: Lefty and Sam, the gangsters, Deepend Dan the Diver, Percival Claude and Cecil, the over polite handymen, and Ali Oop, a Middle Eastern vendor of saucy postcards and other dubious merchandise.

In April the cast were honoured to be invited to perform a special show at Windsor Castle to celebrate Princess Elizabeth's 16th birthday, the first of its kind for a BBC programme. However, the recording was never broadcast. A film version of ITMA was also made starring Handley as the mayor of Foaming at the Mouth, putting on a show to save a bombed theatre.

By the time they had returned to the airwaves in September 1942, Foaming at the Mouth was graced with a war factory. It was never made clear what, if anything, it was producing and even the workers were clueless. The famous Colonel Humphrey Chinstrap made his first appearance, and rapidly became one of the most popular characters. The colonel was a dipsomaniac army officer who turned almost any

Above: RAF pilots relaxing while waiting for their oders during World War II.

74

innocent remark into the offer of a drink with his catchphrase "I don't mind if I do". The following season saw the war factory turned into a spa, a holiday camp and a hotel.

By October 1943, the worst of the air raids were thought to be over, so the BBC Variety Department returned to London. The seventh series saw Handley as the Squire of Much Fiddling. A special edition was broadcast early the following year from the navy base at Scapa Flow. This was followed by episodes allocated to air force (held at the Criterion theatre in London) and the army (from a garrison theatre "somewhere in England").

In September, a new character Mark Time was introduced; elderly and depraved, he answered all questions with "I'll 'ave to ask me Dad". Also Handley's character acquired a domineering secretary Miss Hotchkiss, named after a make of machine gun. On 10 May 1945 the end of the war was celebrated by a special VE edition.

The final ITMA was broadcast on 6 January 1949. Tommy Handley died suddenly of a cerebral haemorrhage three days later.

This song was written for Noel Gay's show *The Little Dog Laughed* which opened in October 1939. It was popular throughout the war, especially after Bud Flanagan and Chesney Allen changed the lyrics to poke fun at the Germans (e.g. Run Adolf, Run Adolf, Run, Run, Run...)

RUN RABBIT RUN

Words by Noel Gay and Ralph Butler.
Music by Noel Gay

Run rabbit – run rabbit –
Run! Run! Run!
Run rabbit – run rabbit –
Run! Run! Run!
So run rabbit – run rabbit –
Run! Run! Run!

Run rabbit – run rabbit –
Run! Run! Run!
Don't give the farmer his fun! Fun! Fun!
He'll get by without his rabbit pie
So run rabbit – run rabbit –
Run! Run! Run!

75

Arthur Askey

Arthur Askey was born in 1900. In 1924 he began his professional career as a music-hall performer. It wasn't until 1938's *Bandwagon*, lasting a full five seasons, that he became a household name in England. In 1937 he made his film debut in *Calling All Stars*, but then in 1939 *Bandwagon* was made into a film and he became a star. A sequel soon followed in which "Big-Hearted" Arthur and co-star Richard "Stinker" Murdoch were evicted from their beloved flat. Film stardom carried Arthur through to the mid-1940s, but it wasn't till 1956 that he starred in another film, *Ramsbottom Rides Again*. He started his own television show *The Arthur Askey Show*, which continued until his retirement. He died in 1982.

He was the first singer to record the song 'Hang Out the Washing on the Siegfried Line'.

The Films of 1939

Adventures of Huckleberry Finn – Richard Thorpe
Babes in Arms – Busby Berkeley
Beau Geste – William A. Wellman
Bronze Buckaroo – Richard C. Kahn
Buck Rogers – Ford I. Beebe
Dark Victory – Edmund Goulding
Daughter of the Tong – Raymond K. Johnson
Daybreak (Le Jour se lève) – Marcel Carne
Destry Rides Again – George Marshall
Devil's Daughter – Arthur Leonard
Double Deal – Arthur Dreifuss
Drums Along the Mohawk – John Ford
Golden Boy – Rouben Mamoulian
Gone With the Wind – Victor Fleming
Gunga Din – George Stevens
Harlem Rides the Range – Richard Kahn
Hunchback of Notre Dame – Wallace Worsley
Jamaica Inn – Alfred Hitchcock
Juarez – William Dieterle
Lying Lips – Oscar Micheaux
Midnight Shadow – George Randol
Moon Over Harlem – Edgar G. Ulmer
Mothers of Today (Hayntike mames) – Henry Lynn
Mr Moto's Last Warning – Norman Foster.
Mr Wong in Chinatown – William Nigh
Mr Smith Goes to Washington – Frank Capra

Whilst in Europe the world was turning grey, the song from the film *The Wizard of Oz* became very popular as it brought a little bit of magic and hope back into people's lives.

Ninotchka – Ernst Lubitsch
Of Mice and Men – Lewis Milestone
Paradise in Harlem – Joseph Seidon
Roaring Twenties – Raoul Walsh
Rules of the Game – Jean Renoir
Stagecoach – John Ford
The Story of the Last Chrysanthemum – Kenji Mizoguchi
Volpone – Maurice Tourneur
Wizard of Oz – Victor Fleming

OVER THE RAINBOW

Written by Harold Arlen and Yip Harburg

*Somewhere ,over the rainbow,
Way up high,
There's a land that I heard of
once in a lullaby.
Somewhere, over the rainbow,
Skies are blue,
And the dreams that you dare to dream
Really do come true.*

*Someday I'll wish upon a star
And wake up where the clouds
are far behind me.
Where troubles melt like lemon drops
Away above the chimney tops
That's where you'll find me.*

*Somewhere over the rainbow,
Bluebirds fly. Birds fly over the rainbow.
Why then ,oh why can't I?
If happy little bluebirds fly
Beyond the rainbow,
Why, oh why, can't I?*

THE WHITE CLIFFS OF DOVER

*Written by Nat Burton
and Walter Kent*

*There'll be bluebirds over the
white cliffs of Dover
Tomorrow, just you wait and see.
There'll be love and laughter and
peace ever after
Tomorrow when the world is free.*

*(The shepherd will tend his sheep)
(The valley will bloom again)
And Jimmy will go to sleep
In his own little room again.*

*There'll be bluebirds over the
white cliffs of Dover.
Tomorrow, just you wait and see
There'll be bluebirds over the
white cliffs of Dover
Tomorrow, just you wait ...and see.*

The Blitz

Herman Goering, Commander of the Luftwaffe, the German air force, targeted London at the beginning of September 1940. He hoped to break the morale of the people of Britain by attacking their capital. He promised Hitler that London, all 800 square miles of it, would be reduced to uninhabitable chaos. Its citizens would flee in terror, blocking the roads, bringing the government to a standstill and Britain would sue for peace. He had at his disposal the largest air force in the world.

Air raid wardens checked that the blackout was effective and being observed by all and ensured that everyone had been issued with a gas mask. They also had to judge the extent and type of damage in their area so that the control centre could send out the appropriate rescue services. Their local knowledge was vital if time was to be saved hunting for survivors trapped beneath debris. They had also to find temporary accommodation for those whose homes had been destroyed during the air raids.

On Sunday 29 December, 1940, a Luftwaffe bombing raid unleashed 100,000 incendiaries onto the capital. The Blitz had begun.

The Civil Defence organisation was the back bone of the home front. The organisation incorporated a vast number of services and civilian voluntary groups.

The most important part of the Civil Defence organisation was its communication system. After the Luftwaffe had dropped their bomb-loads, the speed at which the emergency services were mobilised was crucial. Getting the right sort of aid to the right area (firemen for fires, rescue teams for those trapped in rubble, ambulances for the injured) was the responsibility of those involved.

78

On 13 May 1940, just three days after becoming prime minister, Winston Churchill made one of his most famous speeches. In it, he told the people:

> *"I have nothing to offer but blood, toil, tears and sweat."*

It was characteristic of the British that when, on the following day, Anthony Eden, Secretary for War, announced the formation of the Local Defence Volunteers, better known as the Home Guard or "Dad's Army", 250,000 of them volunteered within 24 hours.

In order to minimise casualties in cities such as London the whole country was divided into areas: evacuation areas, neutral areas and reception areas. The idea was to move children over five years of age, pregnant mothers, mothers with children under five and disabled people away from the danger. They would be safe and big cities would have fewer mouths to feed and fewer injured and dead to deal with in the terrible bombing that was expected.

Some people who remained in London began to sleep in the Underground, where the bombs could not reach them. Others had to move into them because their homes had been bombed out. Tube stations became a "home from home" to many. Performers went and played to them to boost their morale. One of the most popular and most tireless was the loveable George Formby.

79

Above: Winston Churchill.

George Formby

George Formby was born on 26 May 1904 in Wigan, Lancashire. His father was at that time a struggling variety artist, who was soon to become one of the greatest stars of the Edwardian music hall. His father, in his bid to attain success, suffered stress and health problems and Formby was actively discouraged from following in his footsteps. At the age of seven George was sent away to become a jockey.

In 1921, Formby's father died and George returned home from the stables for the funeral. Contrary to his father's wishes his mother Eliza wanted him to keep his father's act alive and the family needed the income. She taught him all she knew of Formby senior's act, and six songs from gramophone records. Less than two months after the death of his father, dressed in his altered stage clothes and using his material, George made his first professional appearance at the Hippodrome cinema, Earlestown, followed by a short tour, during which he said, "I died the death of a dog!". In 1923, George met Beryl Ingham who with her sister May worked as a clog dancing team, "The Two Violets". She was unimpressed by George's unprofessional act. She had been a professional for 10 years, and was one of the most talented dancers in her field. However, she thought he had potential and, after they got married in September 1924, she assumed professional and financial control over George. In June 1926, he made his first records – six acoustic recordings – still imitating his father.

However, under Beryl's guidance, he phased out his father's material and deadpan delivery and introduced a ukulele into his routine, along with a slick, Brylcreemed image and upbeat cheeky numbers full of doubles entendres and catchy tunes.

In September 1929, when he recorded two sides for the Dominion Record Company, his ukulele first appeared on disc. He and Beryl starred together in touring revues during the late 20s. In June 1932, he secured a recording contract with Decca. His first two songs for them were with Jack Hylton and his band – 'Chinese Laundry Blues' and 'Do De O Do'. Another three songs were recorded with Hylton later in the year. Over the next three years he made a further 30 recordings for Decca. In 1935 he moved to Regal-Zonophone and up to 1946 made over 160 titles.

As he became established as a recording artist, George's name began to become known outside the limits of the music hall. He was approached by a small Manchester-based film company and in 1934 made *Boots! Boots!* which included four songs and a clog-dancing sequence with Beryl. Unfortunately, it was appalling and Formby was so disillusioned he swore he would never make another. As a distributor for the film could not be found, Formby went off again around the variety theatres. To everyone's surprise, the film was eventually sold and became a huge success in the north.

In 1935, George made a follow-up film, again with Beryl as co-star, *Off The Dole*. The head of Ealing Studios, whilst visiting the north, saw large queues outside cinemas where both films were showing and signed George up. *No Limit* was the first film George made for Ealing Studios. It was well written, had catchy songs and a strong supporting cast. His part, that of a Lancashire chimney sweep who builds his own motorbike and wins the Manx TT Races, was ideally suited to him. He was a very keen motorcyclist himself and he enjoyed doing his own stunts. The film was very well received and was the start of a run of comedies for Ealing, featuring many of his most popular musical numbers. Some of them featured George up against the enemy.

Under Beryl's shrewd and ruthless management, George Formby became the biggest attraction in British show business, and for six years was the top box-office star, earning over £90,000 a year. At the outbreak of war, he joined the Blackpool Home Guard as a dispatch rider, and launched into an exhausting series of troop concerts. With Beryl as ever at his side, George toured the country raising money for blitzed families, encouraging and sponsoring salvage drives. He also wrote newspaper articles and made broadcasts of a serious and sometimes controversial nature in aid of the war effort.

In addition to this, he toured the battle fronts of North Africa, India, Burma, Malta, Gibraltar and Italy, and was in Normandy less than a week after D-Day, boosting morale. In 1946 he was awarded the OBE for his war services and the personal courage he had shown.

His wartime exertions had left him with a weak heart, but had given him a taste for travel. After the war and until the late-1950s, he appeared in Australia, New Zealand, Canada, South Africa, Denmark, Japan, Sweden and Norway. On 6 March 1961, George Formby died. He was buried, at his own request, beside his father in the Manchester Road Catholic cemetery in Warrington.

HOME GUARD BLUES

The Saint Louis Blues, the Bye Bye Blues
I've had 'em all, the big and the small.
They all were good, you must allow, but
oh brother there's another now.
I've got the Home Guard Blues, I've got
the Home Guard Blues.
On sentry go in the night
If it's wet the water trickles down your
neck to where it tickles,
and the raindrops ooze through your
socks and shoes.
If you're feeling on the black side with
the wind around your earholes
Then you'll get those Home Guard Blues.
I've got the Home Guard Blues, I've got
the Home Guard Blues.
On sentry go in the night
When the Sergeant's wife, a beauty, said
now you must do your duty,
How could I refuse, his wife to amuse.
But she found me rather lacking, and then
said come on get cracking,
Or I'll get those Home Guard Blues.
I've got the Home Guard Blues, I've got
those Home Guard Blues.
On sentry go in the night,
"Who goes there?" I asked a lancer and
got such a filthy answer.
Oh! what words to use, I blushed to
my shoes.
I said "Pass" then sweet as sugar. He
replied "Shut up you blighter".
Now I've got those Home Guard Blues.

Invasion of the Low Countries

On 17 May 1940 the Germans invaded Belgium. Armoured thrusts by the French under de Gaulle, at Laon and by the British at Arras dented but did not block the Panzer advance. By the 20th Heinz Guderian, the Panzer Supreme Commander, was racing along the Somme towards the Channel. Despite fierce resistance from the British 12th and 23rd divisions, the 1st Panzer Division captured Amiens at midday, and the 2nd Division had reached Abbeville and Noyelles at the mouth of the river by evening. They had advanced an incredible 386km in only 11 days. By 22 May, Guderian was striking north to attack the encircled British and French troops in what would become the Dunkirk perimeter.

On 24 May 1940, to the intense frustration of the Panzer generals, Hitler ordered their divisions to halt at Gravelines, South-West of Dunkirk. Why this order was given is still a mystery but it is believed that Hitler did not believe Germany would benefit by bringing Britain to her knees. His aim was British acknowledgement of Germany's position on the Continent. Hitler's hesitation resulted in what has come to be known as "The Miracle of Dunkirk", a massive sea-borne rescue of over 300,000 men from the French coast.

After the evacuation of Dunkirk, General Weygand took stock of his sadly depleted French army. Twenty-four infantry divisions, all three mechanised divisions, two light cavalry divisions and one armoured division had been lost. In addition all but one British division – the 51st Infantry division – had escaped from the Dunkirk beaches. General Weygand considered that if the troops were re-formed they would total 60 divisions as against Germany's 130 divisions. Re-grouping could not possibly be completed until 15 June by which time the enemy would most certainly have attacked.

In the first few months of the war the Allies had ruled supreme in the Mediterranean. Oil supplies passed undisturbed through the Suez canal from the Middle East and British communications with India remained secure. Then on 10 June 1940 Italy entered the war.

On 13 June the Germans, after crossing the River Seine, reached Evreux. As they advanced they pushed the French 10th Army westwards towards Brittany. The remaining troops, exhausted by four days of battle and night marches, also began to withdraw from around Paris. Thus Paris was cleared completely of Allied armies. On 21 June 1940 France surrendered.

Mussolini's invasion of Greece in October 1940 posed an immediate threat to Yugoslavia, not only because of its proximity to Greece but also because of the port of Thessaloniki, to which the Yugoslavs had enjoyed special rights. Crete, the largest island in the Aegean Sea, occupied a central strategic position in the eastern Mediterranean. Suda Bay, one of its three harbours, was the largest harbour in the Mediterranean and an obvious base for naval operations.

It was not looking good strategically for Britain. However, nothing was going to stop morale-boosting entertainment for the troops.

ENSA

In September 1940, *The Manchester Sunday Chronicle* wrote:

"If Goebbels wants to see the effects of German raids on British morale, he ought to be in a theatre while an air-raid alarm is on. A big audience simply revelled in a free after-the-show concert by Max Miller, Vera Lynn, Doris Hare and Tommy Trinder the other night. And they chipped in £15 for a Spitfire."

The Entertainments' National Service Association, or ENSA, was established as early as 1939. In May 1942 it was renamed the Department of National Service, but everyone still referred to it as ENSA. Just like the American USO, ENSA followed the troops all over the war regions in Europe, Africa and the Far East, featuring not only light entertainment artists, but also serious musicians like Yehudi Menuhin and Solomon and Moura Lympany.

One woman known as "The Forces' Sweetheart" captured all their hearts. Her name was Vera Lynn.

Vera Lynn

Born in London's East End in 1917, Vera Lynn began her singing career at the age of seven, performing in local clubs. At age 11, she joined Madame Harris' Kracker Cabaret Kids, a dance troupe, and at 15 became a vocalist with Howard Baker's orchestra.

In 1935 she made her first radio broadcast with the Joe Loss Orchestra and was hired as a vocalist by Charlie Kunz. She also made her first recordings, both with Kunz and anonymously for the Woolworth's Crown label. In 1937 she joined Bert Ambrose's orchestra and remained with them almost exclusively until 1941. In 1939, she married clarinet and tenor sax player Harry Lewis, of the Ambrose band, who also became her manager.

She hosted a BBC radio programme, *Sincerely Yours*, which, with its morale-boosting ballads, became extremely popular with servicemen. She appeared in an armed forces stage revue many times with ENSA and in 1944 made a tour of Burma. She also made three wartime films.

After the war ended, she retired, only to return to show business in 1947, touring and hosting a new radio programme. Her record label, Decca, promoted her in the US

KISS ME GOODNIGHT, SERGEANT MAJOR

Written by Art Noel and Don Pelosi

Kiss me goodnight, Sergeant Major.
Tuck me in my little wooden bed.
We all love you, Sergeant Major
When we hear you baw-ling "Show a leg!".
Don't forget to wake me in the morning
And bring me round a nice hot cup of tea.
Kiss me goodnight, Sergeant Major.,
Sergeant Major, be a mother to me!
Sergeant Major, be a mother to me!

Above: Vera Lynn, "The Forces' Sweetheart".

during the musicians' strike of 1948 and she garnered a US Top 10 hit with 'You Can't Be True, Dear'. She became the first British artist to hit number one on the US charts with 'Auf Wiedersehen, Sweetheart' in 1952. In 1954, she had her first and only British No 1 with 'My Son, My Son'. In 1976, she was made Dame Vera Lynn.

The Battle of Britain

With the surrender of France on 21 June 1940, Hitler was now able to concentrate on the plan to invade Britain, codenamed "Operation Sealion". A successful invasion would only be achieved once control of both the English Channel and the North Sea was won. The key here was not sea power, but air power. Until the RAF was driven from the skies, German landing craft could not cross the Channel in safety. With the Luftwaffe remaining the finest air force in the world and Goering's assurance of its invincibility, Hitler resolved to pit the Luftwaffe against the RAF to secure control of the airways and ultimately control of Britain.

The Fleet Air Arm

The Fleet Air Arm, administered entirely by the Admiralty, began its independent existence on 24 May, 1939, when the Royal Navy took over complete charge of all sea-borne aircraft, whether in aircraft carriers or other warships.

The Battle of the Waves

A pre-war measure by the Admiralty Trade Division had been the establishment in June 1939 of the Defensively Equipped Merchant Ship (DEMS) organisation. Old naval guns and related equipment were collected and stored in the main ports.

U-Boats

The German U-Boat, as in World War I, proved yet again to be a deadly weapon against British ships. Between 9 and 12 September, 1941, 16 British ships were sunk for the loss of only one U-Boat. Although vulnerable to an attack when on the surface, these vessels were efficient and deadly when submerged.

The German Navy adopted "Wolf Pack" tactics, based on the principle of concentration. By operating in an extended search line hundreds of miles of ocean could be covered. This enabled the U-boats to search and attack convoys of ships much more efficiently. It also offered some degree of security for the U-boats by providing too many threats for the escort ships to tackle.

Between 1935 and 1945 Nazi Germany produced 26 different types of U-boat. Germany actually went to war in 1939 with only 57 coastal and ocean-going U-boats. This was due to the fact that the ban on Germany possessing submarines, under the terms of the Treaty of Versailles, made the newly formed German Navy of the 1920s and 1930s concentrate on surface warships. Peak production of this deadly weapon was not reached until the last year of the war.

At the start of the World War II British submarines were used primarily in a reconnaissance role. This work was undertaken in the southern North Sea and near the Norwegian coast beyond the range of aircraft patrols. This work met with relatively little success, though, as there were not enough submarines to cover the area and the winter darkness went on too long for them to be effective in sighting German surface units.

Of all the various sections within the Naval Intelligence Division, the Submarine Tracking Room, was probably the most important. This branch eventually controlled virtually the whole of the anti-submarine warfare and, apart from the odd occasion, very few ever dared to question its judgements. "Active" sonar, the submarine detector commonly called ASDIC (the initials of the Allied Submarine Detection Investigation Committee which had initiated its development in 1917), was basically a transceiver sending out sound impulses and picking up echoes from the objects it struck. It pinpointed U-boats, but echoes also came back from shoals of fish, tidal movements and shifts in the temperature of water.

During the war it was customary for cities, towns and villages, to organise "Warship Weeks" whereby money was raised through National Savings to meet the cost of providing a particular ship. The cities paid for big battleships or aircraft carriers whilst many towns found sufficient money for cruisers or large destroyers.

Merchant shipping was continually at risk during the early years of the war because of the inability of shore-based aircraft to provide more than partial cover over submarine-infested waters. An obvious solution was to provide merchant fleets with portable air cover, in the form of planes based on aircraft carriers. This was the origin of the type of ship named the escort carrier.

Above: Naval chart manoeuvres.

WORLD WAR II, 1939-1945

The Films of 1940

American Matchmaker – Edgar G. Ulmer
Bank Dick – Eddie Cline
Broadway Melody of 1940 – Norman Taurog
Broken Strings – Clarence Muse
Christmas in July – Preston Sturges
Fantasia – Walt Disney
Foreign Correspondent – Alfred Hitchcock
Grapes of Wrath – John Ford
Great Dictator – Charles Chaplin
Great McGinty – Preston Sturges
His Girl Friday – Howard Hawks
Invisible Man Returns – Joe May
Jud Suss – Harlan Veit
Kitty Foyle – Sam Wood
Letter – William Wyler
Long Voyage Home – John Ford
Mark of Zorro – Rouben Mamoulian
Mortal Storm – Frank Borzage
Murder Over New York (Charlie Chan) – Harry Lachman
My Little Chickadee – Eddie Cline
Philadelphia Story – George Cukor
Pinocchio – Walt Disney
Pride & Prejudice – Robert Leonard
Rebecca – Alfred Hitchcock
Stranger on the 3rd Floor – Boris Ingster
Sunday Sinners – Arthur Dreifuss
Thief of Baghdad – Michael Powell (with Ludwig Berger and Tim Whelan)
They Drive by Night – Raoul Walsh

WHEN YOU WISH UPON A STAR

*From: Pinocchio
Written by Leigh Harline
and Ned Washington*

*When you wish upon a star,
Makes no difference who you are,
Anything your heart desires
Will come to you.*

*If your heart is in your dream,
No request is too extreme
When you wish upon a star
As dreamers do.*

*Fate is kind.
She brings to those to love
The sweet fulfillment of
Their secret longing.*

*Like a bolt out of the blue
Fate steps in and sees you through.
When you wish upon a star
Your dreams come true.*

A Nightingale Sang in Berkeley Square

That certain night, the night we met
There was magic abroad in the air.
There were angels dining at the Ritz
And a nightingale sang
in Berkeley Square.

I may be right, I may be wrong,
But I'm perfectly willing to swear
That when you turned and smiled at me
A nightingale sang in Berkeley Square.

The moon that lingered over
London town,
Poor puzzled moon,
he wore a frown.
How could he know we
two were so in love?
The whole darned world seemed
upside down.

The streets of town were
paved with stars.
It was such a romantic affair
And as we kissed and said good-night
A nightingale sang,
A nightingale sang.
I know 'cause I was there
That night in Berkeley Square.

Women At War

Back home it was the women who coped with rationing, clothing coupons, working in munitions factories, becoming Land Army Girls, and the blackout. All this whilst knowing that their husbands, sons, brothers and loved ones were fighting abroad.

Nearly half a million women served in the forces during the World War II. By the time war was declared, some 20,000 women had already volunteered for the auxiliary forces. In the very early days, there was little provision for any form of training. The jobs open to women were limited therefore to those involving skills which female volunteers might be expected to possess already, for example, cooks, orderlies, clerical workers and occasionally as drivers.

In March 1941 Ernest Bevin, Minister for Labour, called on the women of Britain to help the war effort. Many women of all ages found themselves not only in munitions factories, but also in more male-dominated jobs such as aircraft factories. This allowed men to be released into the army, air force and navy. Women could choose to join one of the auxiliary services – the Women's Royal Naval Service (WRNS), the Women's Auxiliary Air Force (WAAF), the Auxiliary Territorial Service (ATS) – or work on the farms, as members of the Women's Land Army (WLA).

'We could do with thousands more like you ..'

JOIN THE WOMEN'S LAND ARMY

shortage of material, older clothes were transformed into modern styles and women's magazines carried tips on how to spend clothes coupons and how to revamp old suits and dresses. Women even converted their husbands' suits into suits to wear themselves as the majority of men were in uniform in the forces.

Heavy blankets were converted into fashionable overcoats and knitting, using old wool, was encouraged. Knitting patterns were produced for slippers, socks and jumpers for all age groups as well as standard patterns for the various services The sewing patterns of the time all had to conform to the same stringent guidelines as shop-purchased clothes, especially on hems, pleats and turn-ups to avoid wastage of material.

British women learned to improvise with make-up and hair products. Gloves, hats and gas masks were a must. Hats could be easily adapted by adding flowers or feathers. Gas masks were a little harder to hide so bags were made to house the cardboard box and gas mask. Some were even incorporated into handbags as a false bottom.

Women's found themselves increasingly in the previously male-dominated arenas of manning anti-aircraft batteries, driving trains and tractors and operating heavy plant etc.

Practical clothing became de rigeur. Trousers or dungarees were worn instead of skirts and headscarves were used to prevent hair getting caught in machines. The government broadcast the slogan "Make do and mend". Owing to the

Even though the bombs were dropping all around the women took great pride in their appearance and indeed saw it as their patriotic duty to ensure they looked their best.

1941

Above: Poster for the Women's Land Army.

'A BIT OF HOME'

RED CROSS & St JOHN
needs your help for
Prisoners of War

The Red Cross

During the war, the British Red Cross Society and the Order of St John conducted their work as a joint body. The function of the war organisations was to supplement the work of the medical branches of the fighting forces, the Ministry of Health and other government authorities by providing all sorts of comforts and amenities that were not within the scope of the official agencies. Their ranks were filled by women.

Above: Recruitment poster for the Red Cross.

The Women's Voluntary Service

In autumn 1938, the home secretary, Sir Samuel Hoare, approached Dowager Lady Reading with a view to recruiting women to help with air raid precautions. By the end of the year the Women's Voluntary Service for Civil Defence was 300,000 strong. The war time plea of "ask the W.V.S. to do it" emphasises the immense variety of tasks undertaken by the W.V.S.

LAND ARMY SONG

Written by C. A. Lejeune

*Back to the land, we must all
lend a hand.
To the farms and the fields we must go.
There's a job to be done,
Though we can't fire a gun
We can still do our bit with the hoe...
Back to the land, with its clay
and its sand,
Its granite and gravel and grit.
You grow barley and wheat
And potatoes to eat,
To make sure that the nation keeps fit...
We will tell you once more
You can help win the war
If you come with us – back to the land.*

One of the many amazing women who contributed much to troop morale was Gracie Fields.

Gracie Fields

Gracie was born on 9 January 1898 over her grandmother's fish and chip shop in Rochdale to Fred and Jenny Stansfield. In her early days she toured in juvenile troupes and worked part-time in a factory. Her career started to climb when she met cockney comedian Archie Pitt. In 1915 they did their first revue together which led to further successes. In 1923 they married.

In 1925 she became a star when Archie Pitt's revue, *Mr Tower of London,* was booked into London's Alhambra theatre by Sir Oswald Stoll. It was a great success and toured for nine years. The couple became very rich. After this West End hit she was to appear in nearly every variety theatre there was, topping the bill wherever she went. Her performances were so popular that often there was standing room only.

In 1931 she made her film debut in *Sally in Our Alley*, which gave her her signature tune 'Sally'. She made a further 15 films, all of which were very successful. By 1937 Gracie was the highest-paid film star in the world. She never enjoyed making films and found difficulty in relating to an invisible audience. Nevertheless, in 1937 she was invited to Hollywood to publicise a contract with 20th Century Fox. She was also presented with "Freedom of the Borough" by her home town of Rochdale, an honour she proudly treasured. By 1938 she was at the height of her popularity and the position she occupied in the public's affection was second only to that of the king and queen. In 1938 she was given the Order of Officer Sister of St John of Jerusalem for her unstinting charity work. She was also awarded the CBE by King George VI for her contribution to the entertainment industry. She toured America, Canada and South Africa.

After making her 1939 film *Shipyard Sally* she developed cancer of the cervix. The newspapers and radio soon made the public aware of her situation. Never before had such adulation and concern been shown to a star, and Gracie received over 250, 000 letters and telegrams from her admirers from all over the world. After the operation she went to her estate at Capri (which she had bought in 1933) to recuperate with her companion Mary Davey and film director Monty Banks. Shortly after her arrival there war was declared. Even though she was still seriously ill, Gracie wanted to do her bit and went with Arthur Askey to entertain the British Expeditionary Force troops in France. Throughout the war she tirelessly visited every war-zone in Europe, the Middle East and the Far East.

91

Above: Gracie Fields.

WORLD WAR II, 1939-1945

In 1940 Gracie and Monty Banks decided to marry. In June 1940 Italy entered the war on the side of Germany. This created a great dilemma for Gracie and her new husband, as he was Italian and was threatened with internment as an enemy alien. To avoid this situation and to protect her marriage she took up the offer of a series of concerts in Canada and America. Suddenly the British press turned on her, accusing her of being a traitor, of taking all her money out of Britain and running away at a time of war. None of this was true; as Winston Churchill pointed out to her, she could do more good for the war effort in the USA than she could do in Great Britain. However the whole episode was very hurtful and made a lasting impression on Gracie as some of her public turned against her. In spite of this, she made hundreds of thousands for the British war effort and returned twice to the United Kingdom, in 1941 and again in 1943.

She died in 1979.

A LASSIE FROM LANCASHIRE

Written by Loraine Hart

She's a lassie from Lancashire,
Just a lassie from Lancashire.
She's a lassie that I love dear, oh! so dear.
Though she dresses in clogs and shawl,
She's the prettiest of them all.
None could be fairer or rarer than Sarah,
My lass from Lancashire.

The Desert Campaign

Whilst the war spread to the Balkan states and Crete, the campaign in North Africa continued unabated. The Italians, humiliated by O'Connor and his "desert rats" had had to be rescued by the German Army. Then on 12 February the great tactician Lieutenant-General Erwin Rommel arrived in Tripoli with the first units of the Afrika Korps. The war in the desert now took on a new dimension.

Between the end of February 1941 and Montgomery's victory at El Alamein in November 1942, the British enjoyed precious little success in the Desert War. With the exception of Crusader in late 1941, operations failed and commanders came and went with regularity but few advantages were gained.

America Enters the War

By mid-summer the US was convoying merchant vessels as far as Iceland and when in October the *Reuben James*, an escort destroyer, was torpedoed and sunk, the US Navy was permitted to declare "war" on the U-boats attacking American-escorted convoys. Two months later on 7 December 1941, Japan attacked the American fleet in Pearl Harbor. The following day Congress declared war on Japan. Three days later Germany and Italy declared war on the United States, and she was caught up in what had seemed in 1939 to be an unpleasant piece of European politics.

92

The Films of 1941

Big Store – Charles Riesner
Blood of Jesus – Spencer Williams
Citizen Kane – Orson Welles
Dumbo – Walt Disney
High Sierra – Raoul Walsh
How Green was My Valley – John Ford
I Wake Up Screaming – Bruce Humberstone
Lady Eve – Preston Sturges
Maltese Falcon – John Huston
Meet John Doe – Frank Capra
Mr and Mrs Smith – Alfred Hitchcock
Ohm Kruger – Hans Steinhoff
Phantom of Chinatown – (Mr Wong detective story) Phil Rosen
Sleeping Beauty – Walt Disney
Sullivan's Travels – Preston Sturges
Suspicion – Alfred Hitchcock
Wolf Man – George Waggner

ONCE UPON A DREAM

From: Sleeping Beauty
Written by Sammy Fain and Jack Lawrence

*I know you, I walked with you
once upon a dream.
I know you, the gleam in your eyes is
so familiar a gleam.
Yet I know it's true that visions are
seldom all they seem
But if I know you, I know what you do.
You love me at once, the way you did
once upon a dream.*

*But if I know you, I know what you do
You love me at once
The way you did once upon a dream.
I know you, I walked with you once
upon a dream.
I know you, the gleam in your eyes is so
familiar a gleam.*

*And I know it's true that visions are
seldom all they seem
But if I know you, I know what you do.
You love me at once, the way you did
once upon a dream.*

BOOGIE WOOGIE BUGLE BOY

*He was a famous trumpet man
from out Chicago way.
He had a boogie style that no one else
could play.
He was the top man at his craft
But then his number came up and he was
gone with the draft.
He's in the army now, blowing reveille.
He's the boogie woogie bugle boy of
Company B.
They made him blow a bugle for his
Uncle Sam.
It really brought him down because
he could not jam.
The captain seemed to understand
Because the next day the cap' went out
and drafted a band
And now the company jumps when
he plays reveille.
He's the boogie woogie bugle boy of
Company B.
A-toot, a-toot, a-toot-diddelyada-toot
He blows it eight-to-the-bar,
in boogie rhythm.
He can't blow a note unless the bass and
guitar is playing with him.
He makes the company jump when
he plays reveille.
He's the boogie woogie bugle boy of
Company B.
He was our boogie woogie bugle boy of
Company B.
And when he plays boogie woogie*

*bugle he was busy as a "bzzz" bee
And when he plays he makes the company
jump eight-to-the-bar.
He's the boogie woogie bugle boy of
Company B.
Toot-toot-toot, toot-diddelyada,
toot-diddelyada
Toot, toot, he blows it eight-to-the-bar.
He can't blow a note if the bass and
guitar isn't with him
And the company jumps when
he plays reveille.
He's the boogie woogie bugle boy of
Company B.
He puts the boys asleep with
boogie every night
And wakes 'em up the same way
in the early bright.
They clap their hands and stomp their feet
Because they know how he plays when
someone gives him a beat.
He really breaks it up when he plays
reveille.
He's the boogie woogie bugle boy of
Company B.
Da-doo-da da-doo-da-da da
Da-doo-da da-doo-da-da da
Da-doo-da da-doo-da-da da
Da-doo-da da-doo-da-da
And the company jumps
when he plays reveille.
He's the boogie woogie bugle boy of
Company B!*

Dancing

Dancing was never more popular than during the World War II and there were many people who literally danced their way through it. Dance halls provided a refuge from the bleak realities of war. They were places of innocent pleasure, where the anxieties and fears of the outside world could be forgotten for a short while. Many lonely servicemen, often only on 48-hour leave before returning to the Front, found love and comfort there. The dance halls attracted huge crowds, some with as many as 10,000 dancers packed into a single hall. Dancing was so popular that the bigger dance halls ran four sessions a day: morning, afternoon and two evening sessions. Members of the forces were admitted half price. Establishments like the Hammersmith Palais in London echoed the famous Windmill theatre's boast that it never closed.

When the Americans arrived, they brought with them nylons, cigarettes and "candy", intent on spreading goodwill over the whole country. There was some hostility towards them for joining the fray late – the common jibe about them was that they were "overpaid, oversexed and over here".

However, they brought something with them that was never to be forgotten and that was their music. They also brought two new dances – the Jitterbug and the Jive. Jitterbug competitions soon flourished in the dance halls. The music they brought with them dramatically changed the style of dancing.

Whereas before, dancing had been graceful, with set steps to follow, after American music arrived it was characterised by wild gyrations to fit the music.

Although he was only in Britain for six months, one man had a huge influence on Britain's wartime music. His sound is still reverberating around the world in the 21st century. This man was Glenn Miller.

Glenn Miller

Glenn Miller was born 1 March 1904 in Clarinda, Indiana. Early on in his musical career, Miller had worked at a variety of musical jobs and played a jazz trombone. He was a sideman in travelling "road bands" as well as a member of New York theatrical "pit bands". He also authored a significant quantity of arrangements and original tunes including his theme song 'Moonlight Serenade'.

Miller always felt that he was not a very good trombonist, certainly not on a par with the likes of Tommy Dorsey or Jack Teagarden. In fact, he played a reasonably "hot" slide trombone, and can be heard in the Pollack orchestra, and the original Dorsey Brothers band of the early 1930s but after he achieved fame he rarely

soloed. In the mid- to late-1930s, Miller was also the backbone – and often, the behind-the-scenes leader and arranger – of bands that were fronted by John Scott Trotter and cowboy actor/singer Smith Ballew. He had been greatly influenced by Jimmie Lunceford's musicianship style and was also a disciplinarian who drilled his orchestra to perfection.

In 1937 he formed his own orchestra which had a few hotel bookings, radio dates and some recordings for Brunswick, but their "sound" was like many other bands of the time. After an engagement at the Raymor Ballroom in Bridgeport, Connecticut, Miller returned to

New York and disbanded the group in January, 1938. The band included Pee Wee Erwin and Charlie Spivak on trumpets, Hal MacIntyre and Jerry Jerome on saxophones, Irving Fazola on clarinet and Miller's close friend, Chummy MacGregor, on piano.

By March/April, 1938, Miller had formed a new orchestra which was to become the core of the Miller band and key to the Miller "sound", that of the clarinet lead, with tenor saxophone (or saxophones) playing the same melody one octave lower than the clarinet. MacGregor was still on piano, Hal MacIntyre played alto, Tex Benecke arrived as tenor sax, Willie Schwartz arrived to play clarinet and Ray Eberle was the male singer.

Above: Glenn Miller and his orchestra.

In June, 1938, Miller was performing at the Paradise Restaurant in New York City, and his music was piped to the nation via NBC radio broadcasts. After trying several female "songbirds", Miller hired Marion Hutton, the sister of Hollywood star Betty Hutton, around September 1938. By early 1939, the band was under recording contract to Bluebird (RCA), and booked for a long stay at the Meadowbrook Ballroom in Cedar Grove, New Jersey. By mid-1939, they were performing at the Glen Island Casino in New Rochelle, New York and their music continued to be broadcast over NBC, adding further to their popularity.

On 6 October, the Miller band, along with other orchestras, performed at Carnegie Hall. Their popularity growing, the band launched their Chesterfield Show broadcasts in December 1939, and began a long stay at the Café Rouge of the Hotel Pennsylvania in New York City in January 1940. The Modernaires vocal group came on board in early 1941. By March, the orchestra was in Hollywood doing the filming and soundtrack work for the 20th Century Fox film *Sun Valley Serenade*. It starred Miller, the band, skater Sonja Henie and John Payne. A year later, they were back at Fox for their second film, *Orchestra Wives*, which featured George Montgomery, Ann Rutherford and Carole Landis. Billy May and Ray Anthony, who would later go on to lead their own orchestras, were in the Miller trumpet section. During this period, May was doing a lot of arrangements for the band, including his beautiful orchestration for the opening of 'Serenade in Blue'. One of the songs from the movie, 'Chattanooga Choo Choo', became the first million-seller. RCA Victor presented Miller with a gold-plated version of the record to commemorate the event and gold records have been used to recognise bestsellers since then. When World War II erupted, Miller gave a series of Saturday afternoon performances at various military camps across the country. These were broadcast as the *Sunset Serenade* shows, the first of which was aired on 30 August 1941.

By 1942, the band was at the peak of its success and popularity, and Miller was definitely making substantial profits from recordings, broadcasts and personal appearances. However, Miller felt a need to do more for the United States' war effort and joined the military. The last engagement of Miller's civilian orchestra was on 26 September 1942 at the Central theatre in Passaic, New Jersey, only four and a half years after it started. They performed their most popular songs, including 'In the Mood', 'Moonlight Cocktail', 'I've Got a Gal in Kalamazoo' and their 'Moonlight Serenade' theme for the last time.

Sadly Major Glenn Miller died in an airplane crash during the war. Tex Benecke, his first chair sax-man and vocalist, took over leadership of the band and they toured far and wide, remaining active for many more years in honour of their first leader.

IN THE MOOD

Words by Andy Razaf, music by Joe Garland

Who's the lovin' daddy with the beautiful eyes?
What a pair o' lips, I'd like to try 'em for size.
I'll just tell him, "Baby, won't you swing it with me".
Hope he tells me maybe, what a wing it will be.
So, I said politely, "Darlin' may I intrude?"
He said, "Don't keep me waitin' when I'm in the mood".

First I held him lightly and we started to dance.
Then I held him tightly – what a dreamy romance.
And I said, "Hey, baby, it's a quarter to three.
There's a mess of moonlight, won't-cha share it with me?"
"Well", he answered, "Baby, don't-cha know that it's rude
To keep my two lips waitin' when they're in the mood".

In the mood, that's what he told me,
In the mood, and when he told me,
In the mood, my heart was skippin'.
It didn't take me long to say
"I'm in the mood now".
In the mood for all his kissin',
In the mood his crazy lovin',
In the mood what I was missin'.
It didn't take me long to say
"I'm in the mood now".

So, I said politely, "Darlin' may I intrude?"
He said, "Don't keep me waitin' when I'm in the mood".
"Well", he answered, "Baby, don't-cha know that it's rude
To keep my two lips waitin' when they're in the mood?"

Who's the lovin' daddy with the beautiful eyes?
What a pair o' lips, I'd like to try 'em for size.
I'll just tell him, "Baby, won't you swing it with me".
Hope he tells me maybe, what a wing it will be.
So, I said politely, "Darlin' may I intrude?"
He said, "Don't keep me waitin' when
I'm in the mood".

First I held him lightly and we started to dance
Then I held him tightly – what a dreamy romance.
And I said, "Hey, baby, it's a quarter to three.
It's a mess of moonlight, won't-cha share it with me?"
"Well", he answered, "Baby, don't-cha know that it's rude
To keep my two lips waitin' when they're in the mood?"

During World War II, many venues had to close due to wartime restrictions, but many dance bands managed to stay together and the music, a reminder of home and the sweetheart left behind, went overseas with the troops. Many of the bandsmen that joined the armed forces managed to stay together in regimental bands, playing in aircraft hangars, deckside on ships, in post canteens and overseas bases.

The government also supported CEMA (the Council for the Encouragement of Music) which provided funds to small groups, to symphony orchestras and to theatre companies. Bevin had encouraged ENSA to play less formal and more morale-boosting music for the factory workers back home. At the same time the armed forces bands began to move away from strictly military music to play at dance halls themselves.

One of the most popular of these bands was called The Squadronaires.

The Squadronaires

The Squadronaires were formed during World War II and, as the name suggests, consisted of members of the RAF who were originally drawn from the sidemen of Bert Ambrose's band.

For most of the war up to 1945, the line-up consisted of:
Tommy McQuater, Archie Craig, Clinton French on trumpets; George Chisholm and Eric Breeze on trombones; Tommy

Bradbury, Harry Lewis (Vera Lynn's husband), Jimmy Durrant, Andy McDevitt, Cliff Townshend (father of Peter Townshend of The Who) on saxophone; Ronnie Aldrich on piano; Sid Colin on guitar; Arthur Maden on bass (who was also the band's manager); Jock Cummings on drums; and Jimmy Miller on vocals and also acting as band leader.

In 1945, Jimmy Watson (trumpet) replaced Clinton "Froggy" French and Monty Levy (alto saxophone) replaced Harry Lewis. In 1950 Ronnie Aldrich, an arranger, took over as leader and the band was renamed Ronnie Aldrich and the Squadronaires. The line-up then was:

Ron Simmonds, Gracie Cole and Archie Craig on trumpets; Ric Kennedy and Bill Geldard on trombones; Cliff Townshend, Monty Levy, Andy McDevitt, Cyril Reubens and Ken Kiddier on saxophones; Don Innes on piano; Andy Reveley on bass; Tommy Cairns on drums; Roy Edwards, and Andy Reveley on vocals.

Later on Gracie Cole and her husband Bill Geldard were replaced by Terry Lewis on trumpet and Johnny Keating on trombone. In 1964 The Squadronaires disbanded.

One of the most famous dances during World War II, not just in the dance halls but in the streets as well, was the Lambeth Walk.

LAMBETH WALK

Written by E. Maschwitz

Any time you're Lambeth way,
Any evening, any day,
You'll find us all
Doin' the Lambeth Walk.

Every little Lambeth gal,
With her little Lambeth pal,
You'll find 'em all
Doin' the Lambeth Walk.

Everything free and easy,
Do as you darn well pleasy.
Why don't you make your way there?
Go there, stay there.

Once you get down Lambeth way,
Ev'ry ev'ning, ev'ry day,
You'll find yourself
Doin' the Lambeth Walk.

The Eighth Army

The Eighth Army was officially formed on 26 September 1941. It was made up of the remnants of General Wavell's Army of the Nile (1940) and General Sir Alan Cunningham was made its commander. In November 1941 the Eighth Army's first offensive was launched in the Western Desert.

Operation Torch

The largest amphibious force the world had yet known assembled off the North African coast late on 7 November 1942. More than 500 ships, ranging from cargo vessels to passenger liners, had been pressed into service to carry around 107,000 men and thousands of tonnes of weapons and supplies, and land them on the beaches of Morocco and Algeria.

Tunisia

Having been defeated by the Eighth Army at El Alamein, Field Marshal Rommel retreated during November as fast as he could to Tunisia, in the hope that he would be able to inflict a crushing defeat there on the recently arrived American and British forces under General Eisenhower. Because of the agreed plan for

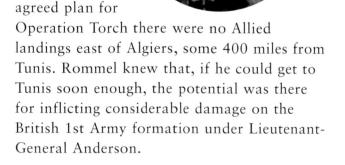

Operation Torch there were no Allied landings east of Algiers, some 400 miles from Tunis. Rommel knew that, if he could get to Tunis soon enough, the potential was there for inflicting considerable damage on the British 1st Army formation under Lieutenant-General Anderson.

WEARS A PAIR OF SILVER WINGS

Written by Eric Maschwitz and Michael Carr

Some people say he's just a crazy guy.
To me he means a million other things,
For he's the one who taught
this happy heart of mine to fly.
He wears a pair of silver wings
And though it's pretty tough,
the job he does above,
I wouldn't have him change it for a king.

An ordinary fellow in a uniform I love.
He wears a pair of silver wings.
Why, I'm so full of pride
when we go walking
Every time he's home on leave.
He with those wings on his tunic
And me with my heart on my sleeve.

But when I'm left alone
and we are far apart
I sometimes wonder
what tomorrow brings
For I adore that crazy guy who taught
my happy heart
To wear a pair of silver wings.
For I adore that crazy guy who taught
my happy heart
To wear a pair of silver wings.

101

Above: Field Marshal Rommel.

WHEN THE LIGHTS
GO ON AGAIN
ALL OVER THE WORLD

Written by Eddie Seller,
Sol Marcus
and Bennie Benjamin

When the lights go on again all over the world,
And the boys are home again all over the world,
And rain or snow is all that may fall from the skies above,
A kiss won't mean "goodbye" but "hello to love".

When the lights go on again all over the world,
And the ships will sail again all over the world,
Then we'll have time for things like wedding rings
and free hearts will sing,
When the lights go on again all over the world.

The Films of 1942

Bambi – David Hand
Casablanca – Michael Curtiz
Cat People – Jacques Tourneur
Flying Tigers – David Miller
Forty-Seven Ronin – Kenji Mizoguchi
Holiday Inn – Mark Sandrich
Magnificent Ambersons – Orson Welles
Now, Voyager – Irving Rapper
Obsession (Ossessione) – Luchino Visconti

Oxbow Incident – William A. Wellman
Palm Beach Story – Preston Sturges
Saboteur – Alfred Hitchcock
Shadow of a Doubt – Alfred Hitchcock
Star Spangled Rhythm – George Marshall
This Gun for Hire – Frank Tuttle
To Be Or Not to Be – Ernst Lubitsch
Why We Fight – Frank Capra *et al.*
In Which We Serve – Noel Coward and David Lean.

By mid-1943 it was clear to the leaders of the three senior Allied powers that Germany and Japan were losing the war. Each of those leaders, Roosevelt, Churchill and Stalin, therefore, began to speculate on the attitudes of the others to the post-war world. Roosevelt and his advisers began to think once more as an isolationist government, while seeing the potential for world power. Washington held a deep mistrust of the extent to which Britain was committed to an invasion of Europe across the English Channel – the operation known as "Overlord". Twice already, Britain had deferred a major landing in northern Europe. Roosevelt, therefore, wanted "Overlord" to have an American commander.

The Merchant Navy At War

At the outbreak of war there were about 21.25 million tonnes of merchant shipping registered in Britain. The merchantmen were the critical element in the struggle. It was these ships upon which men, women and children and every uniformed serviceman depended for survival. They carried food, raw materials and despatches of military forces.

Merchant Aircraft Carriers

By June 1943, although German submarines had virtually been withdrawn from the North Atlantic convoy route, it was still deemed necessary to continue close naval support from escort vessels. Air cover where feasible remained vital. By the end of September 1942 the range of air cover available from Iceland had been increased to 800 miles. In October 1942, the Admiralty ordered that six grain ships, which were then under construction, to be adapted to Merchant Aircraft Carriers or MAC ships, in order to bridge the gap in the Atlantic where shore-based aircraft could not operate. Six tankers were also fitted out with flight decks.

The world has never seen a man quite like Noel Coward. As a writer he could knock off a hit show in a matter of days, as an actor his career spanned five decades and as a cabaret performer he won the hearts of a whole new generation. He was, undoubtedly, a star.

103

Above: By mid-1943 it was clear to the leaders of the three senior Allied powers that Germany and Japan were losing the war.

Noel Coward

Noel Coward was born in Teddington, England, in 1899 to Violet and Arthur Coward. He was encouraged by his ambitious mother and by the age of 12 had made his first professional appearance on the stage. A couple of years later he had his first encounter with the irrepressible Gertrude Lawrence when they appeared together in the play *Hannele*. The stage was set.

In 1924 Coward starred in the first production of his play *The Vortex*, an event which was to alter his life dramatically and propel him into the public eye as a writer and star. The play dealt with the scandalous issue of drug abuse and caused the Lord Chamberlain to declare one particular scene to be revolting in the last degree. Coward had written over 15 plays including *Hay Fever*, *Private Lives* and *Cavalcade* by his mid-30s and was already the subject of a number of biographies. In 1930 Coward starred with Gertrude Lawrence in *Private Lives* and captured the glamorous essence of his generation. With the outbreak of the World War II the "balconies and cocktails" image fell out of fashion and by the 1950s Coward had turned to the world of cabaret to earn his living.

This shift in his career was kick-started by his cabaret show at The Desert Inn in Las Vegas. The Vegas show was given a particularly special boost by Frank Sinatra. Sinatra travelled from Hollywood to see the show and then went on to announce on national radio, "If you want to hear how songs should be sung, get the hell over to The Desert Inn!" Four weeks later Coward left The Desert Inn a star reborn. As an added bonus there was a live-recorded album of the show which, 45 years later, has yet to go out of print.

In 1942 his film *In Which We Serve* earned Coward an Oscar nomination. As a writer he went on to produce such classics as *Brief Encounter*, but his career as a film actor is perhaps more notable for its "might-have-beens". When approached to play the king in *The King and I* he politely declined and pointed Rodgers and Hammerstein in the direction of a little-known young actor called Yul Brynner; when offered the part of Professor Higgins in *My Fair Lady* he refused, and the part was then immortalised by Rex Harrison; he was asked to take the role of Colonel Nicholson in *The Bridge on the River Kwai* but turned it down – Alec Guinness later won an Oscar in the role; and finally the part of Harry Lime in *The Third Man* was refused by Coward before being snapped up by the young Orson Welles.

Above: Noel Coward.

WORLD WAR II, 1939-1945

In 1970 he received a knighthood. His failing health was evident at the ceremony and three years later he died at home in his beloved Jamaica.

Two of his most well known war songs were the ironic 'Don't Let's Be Beastly to the Germans' and – directly aimed at the Ministry of Defence – 'Could You Please Oblige Us With a Bren Gun?'.

COULD YOU PLEASE OBLIGE US WITH A BREN GUN?

Could you please oblige us with
a Bren gun?
Or, failing that, a hand grenade would do.
We've got some ammunition,
In a rather damp condition
And Mayor Huss
Has an arquebus
That was used in Waterloo.
With the vicar's stirrup pump, a pitchfork
and a spade,
It's rather hard to guard an aerodrome.
So if you can't oblige us with a
Bren gun,
The Home Guard might as well go home.

The Warsaw Concerto

The *Warsaw Concerto* was the theme music of the 1941 British movie called *Dangerous Moonlight*. Anton Walbrook starred as a Polish pianist who escapes from the Nazis, only to lose his memory after flying in the Battle of Britain. His emotional performance of the *Warsaw Concerto* as the bombs rained down around him symbolised for many the spirit of resistance to Hitler. The music by Richard Addinsell also helped to bridge a culture gap for many cinema-goers as it was their first taste of classical music. The theme became an instant success all over the world.

USO

Like ENSA the American USO (United Services Organization) sent thousands of performers into the field to entertain the troops. Between them they employed around 10,000 entertainers. Their effect on the morale of servicemen cannot be overestimated. By the end of the war they had performed before a combined audience of over 172 million.

One British-born entertainer travelled thousands of miles between war zones with his troop of entertainers, bringing laughter to bases in far off places. His name was, appropriately, Bob Hope.

105

Bob Hope

Bob Hope was born Leslie Townes Hope on 29 May 1903, in Eltham, England. His family moved to Cleveland, Ohio when he was four. He began performing in vaudeville in the 1920s and made his Broadway debut in 1933 with the musical *Roberta*, in which he met his beloved wife Dolores Reade. In 1935 he appeared in the Ziegfeld Follies and starred with Ethel Merman in a production of Cole Porter's *Red Hot and Blue*. He also hosted a popular radio show on NBC, which lasted from 1938 until the 1950s.

In 1938, Hope moved to Hollywood to pursue a film career, his first film being *The Big Broadcast of 1938*. In 1940 he made the first in a series of *Road to...* films, alongside Bing Crosby and Dorothy Lamour. Other notable films include *The Cat and the Canary* (1939), *The Ghost Breakers* (1940), *My Favorite Brunette*, *The Paleface* (1948), *Sorrowful Jones* (1949) and *The Lemon Drop Kid* (1951).

Hope earned the title "USO's Ambassador of Good Will" as during World War II and both the Korean and Vietnam wars, and even in peacetime, he entertained the troops whilst touring with a number of USO shows. From 1953 to 1994 he hosted an annual Christmas TV special which was broadcast to US troops around the world.

Over the course of his career Hope has received a number of awards: three honorary Academy Awards, the Academy's Jean Hersholt Humanitarian Award, the prestigious Kennedy Center Honors for Lifetime Achievement, and in 1998 he received an honorary knighthood from Queen Elizabeth II.

He still makes the occasional appearance to this day.

The Films of 1943

Baron Muenchhausen (Munchhausen) – Josef Von Baky
Bataan – Tay Garnett
Cabin in the Sky – Vincente Minnelli
Le Corbeau (The Raven) – Henri-Georges Clouzot
Day of Wrath (Vredens dag) – Carl Dreyer
December 7th: the Pearl Harbor Story – John Ford
Eternal Return – Jean Cocteau
Five Graves to Cairo – Billy Wilder
Guadalcanal Diary – Lewis Seiler
Gung Ho! – Ray Enright
Hangmen Also Die – Fritz Lang
Meshes of the Afternoon – Maya Deren
Miracle of Morgan's Creek – Preston Sturges
Paracelsus – G.W. Pabst
Phantom Lady – Robert Siodmak
Phantom of the Opera – Arthur Lubin
Seventh Victim – Mark Robson
So Proudly We Hail – Mark Sandrich
Stormy Weather – Andrew Stone
Where Is My Man Tonight? – Spencer Williams

THANKS FOR THE MEMORY

Written by Ralph Rainger and Leo Robin

Thanks for the memory
Of sentimental verse,
Nothing in my purse,
And chuckles
When the preacher said
For better or for worse.
How lovely it was.

Thanks for the memory
Of Schubert's Serenade,
Little things of jade
And traffic jams
And anagrams
And bills we never paid.
How lovely it was.

We who could laugh over big things
Were parted by only a slight thing.
I wonder if we did the right thing?
Oh, well, that's life, I guess.
I love your dress.

Thanks for the memory
Of faults that you forgave,
Of rainbows on a wave,
And stockings in the basin
When a fellow needs a shave.
Thank you so much.

Thanks for the memory
Of tinkling temple bells,
Alma mater yells
And Cuban rum
And towels from
The very best hotels.
Oh how lovely it was.

Thanks for the memory
Of cushions on the floor,
Hash with Dinty Moore,
That pair of gay pajamas
That you bought
And never wore.

We said goodbye with a highball,
Then I got as high as a steeple,
But we were intelligent people,
No tears, no fuss,
Hooray for us.

Strictly entre nous,
Darling, how are you?
And how are all
Those little dreams
That never did come true?

Awfully glad I met you,
Cheerio and toodle-oo.
Thank you,
Thank you so much.

I'LL BE SEEING YOU

Written by Irving Kahal and Sammy Fain

*I'll be seeing you in all the
old familiar places
That this heart of mine embraces
all day through.
In that small café,
the park across the way,
The children's carousel,
the chestnut trees,
the wishing well.*

*I'll be seeing you in every
lovely summer's day,
In everything that's light and gay
I'll always think of you that way.
I'll find you in the mornin' sun,
And when the night is new,
I'll be looking at the moon,
But I'll be seeing you.*

Monte Cassino

The key to the defence of Rome was the little town of Cassino lying on the River Rapido, dominated by the historic Benedictine monastery atop the 1,693-foot massif of Monte Cassino itself. Known as Monastery Hill to the Allies, this was the main obstacle that lay in the path of the British Eighth and US Fifth Armies during the winter of 1943–4.

The Advance on Rome

The advance from the toe of Italy after the landings at Salerno had been slow. By the end of 1943, it had practically ground to a halt, with particularly horrific problems at Cassino. The stalemate, and the underlying Allied conviction that Rome was the psychologically important target in Italy for both sides, brought forward a number of Allied proposals, with Churchill's idea for "Operation Shingle" eventually emerging as the accepted plan. This was to be a swift strike for Rome following a beach landing at Anzio. The success of this plan would also ensure that German supply lines to Cassino would be severed.

D-Day

Just after midnight on 5/6 June 1944 one of the most complex and intricate operations in the history of warfare went ahead on the orders of the Allied Supreme Commander, General Eisenhower.

Over a quarter of a million men were taking part in the operation. Nearly 5,000 ships were afloat, each with a specific task to perform. In the air squadrons of fighter aircraft kept the skies clear of enemy aircraft. Transport aircraft numbering 1,200 were carrying 20,000 paratroopers whilst gliders were carrying more men and materials to their destinations. Operation Overlord had begun. As well as glider and parachute landings there were assaults on five separate beaches. During the week

following the D-Day landings, Rommel and his depleted Seventh Army failed to contain the Allied beach-head and drive the invasion back to the sea. Rommel knew he was beaten and that Germany had little chance of anything but defeat.

As the most popular singer and one of the most successful movie stars of all time, Bing Crosby was very appealing. His relaxed, likeable, "regular guy next door" charm won him a devoted wartime audience.

Above: The Normandy Landings.

Bing Crosby

Bing Crosby was born Harry Lillis Crosby on 2 May 1904 in Tacoma, Washington. He was nicknamed "Bing" after a popular comic-strip character from *The Bingville Bugle*. He started his musical career as part of The Rhythm Boys, who made their film debut in legendary bandleader Paul Whiteman's *The King of Jazz* in 1930.

He then appeared in a series of two-reel comedies produced by Mack Sennett, often playing an easy-going crooner. In 1932, after a series of radio appearances and a record-breaking run on stage at New York's famed Paramount theatre, he became a star. He then starred in *The Big Broadcast of 1932* in which he introduced his theme song 'Where the Blue of the Night'.

In 1940, he made *The Road to Singapore* with Bob Hope and Dorothy Lamour, the first in a series of seven classic *Road to…* films.

During World War II, Crosby entertained the troops at home and abroad. Although 'Silent Night' was the most popular song he ever recorded, the most popular song of the war was Irving Berlin's 'White Christmas', introduced by Crosby in the film *Holiday Inn* (1942). As sung by Crosby, it embodied the overwhelming nostalgia induced by the war's separation of loved ones better than any other piece of music.

In 1944 Crosby won an Oscar for Best Actor for his portrayal of Father O'Malley in *Going My Way*, and was nominated in 1945 for *The Bells of St Mary's* and in 1954 for *The Country Girl*. He also received 14 song nominations, four of which won Oscars.

He died in 1977.

WHITE CHRISTMAS

Written by Irving Berlin

I'm dreaming of a white Christmas,
Just like the ones I used to know,
Where the treetops glisten,
and children listen
To hear sleigh bells in the snow.

I'm dreaming of a white Christmas
With every Christmas card I write.
May your days be merry and bright
And may all your Christmases be white.

I'm dreaming of a white Christmas
With every Christmas card I write.
May your days be merry and bright
And may all your Christmases be white.

Above: Bing Crosby.

WORLD WAR II, 1939-1945

Anne Shelton

Anne Shelton was born in Dulwich, South London in 1928. She commenced her singing career at the age of 13. Having successfully auditioned for Bert Ambrose, she stayed with his band for six years. In 1943 she gained her own solo recording contract. Her first broadcast was from the Mayfair Hotel.

In 1942 Anne started touring army, navy and air force bases all over the country. The BBC, quick to recognise Anne's popularity with the armed forces, soon gave her a special programme entitled *Calling Malta* – Malta was besieged during the war – which ran for five years. At the same time another programme, *Introducing Anne*, was beamed to North Africa and used to counteract the German propaganda put over to Allied troops.

When Glenn Miller's orchestra arrived in England in 1944, Glenn asked if Anne would sing with his orchestra. Anne took this as a great compliment and did six shows with the maestro. One of them was recorded for Anne on a number of "V" discs.

V-discs were unique because they were the only live recordings made in the USA (and at overseas shows) exclusively for GIs during the recording ban from August 1942 to November 1944. Many of the artists who made V-discs were under contract to different recording companies.

Under normal conditions they could never perform together because of their contractual obligations, yet V-disc staff were able to get together artists who performed "once in a lifetime" sessions for the V-disc program.

In December 1944 Glenn Miller was asked to go to Versailles for a concert. He invited Anne to join him, but her mother reminded her that she had other commitments in England, so she stayed behind thereby escaping the plane crash that claimed the life of Miller.

The same year Bing Crosby arrived in England to entertain the American forces and asked Anne to do a show with him for the troops. On 27 August 1944, Bing and Anne recorded the *Variety Bandbox* radio show at Queensberry All-Services Club, with Tommy Handley. It was broadcast on 3 September. Afterwards Anne and Bing gave an audience of 4,000 a show in which they sang two duets, 'Easter Parade' and 'I'll Get By'.

During the Berlin airlift of 1948-1949, "the boys" were asked who they would like to entertain them. They were told that only one artist could get on the airlift – they chose Anne Shelton. So in went Anne on a plane full of mail and coal. She did 12 shows in three days, one show being staged in Hitler's own theatre in Berlin.

In 1949 Anne had two hits in the USA –
'Be Mine' and 'Galway Bay'. In 1951 she
toured America, returning to England just
in time for Christmas.

On 21 September 1956 Anne reached No 1
with her most famous song 'Lay Down
Your Arms'.

She continued to have a successful career
and worked for many charitable societies
over the next four decades. On 27 July
1994 she gave her final performance for
the Not Forgotten Association at
Buckingham Palace. Four days later she
passed away in her sleep.

Anne's signature tune was 'Lili Marlene'.
Anne successfully competed with the
German version and became known as the
Lili Marlene Girl.

Lili Marlene

'Lili Marlene' was based on a poem written
by German soldier Hans Leip during World
War I and published in 1937. In 1938 it was
set to music by Norbert Schultze and was
recorded just before the war. It became a
favourite of the Germans when it was
broadcast to the Afrika Korps in 1941.

LILI MARLENE

Underneath the lantern by the barrack gate,
Darling I remember the way you used to wait.
'Twas there that you whispered tenderly,
That you loved me,
You'd always be,
My Lili of the lamplight,
My own Lili Marlene.

Time would come for roll call,
Time for us to part,
Darling I'd caress you and press you to my heart,
And there 'neath that far off lantern light,
I'd hold you tight,
We'd kiss "good-night",
My Lili of the lamplight,
My own Lili Marlene.

Orders came for sailing
somewhere over there,
All confined to barracks
was more than I could bear;
I knew you were waiting in the street,
I heard your feet,
But could not meet,
My Lili of the lamplight,
My own Lili Marlene.

Resting in a billet
just behind the line,
Even tho' we're parted your lips are close to mine;
You wait where that lantern softly gleams,
Your sweet face seems to haunt my dreams,
My Lili of the lamplight,
My own Lili Marlene.

LILI MARLENE (GERMAN VERSION)

Words by Hans Leip; Music by Norbert Schultze

Vor der Kaserme vor dem großen Tor
stand eine Lanterne
und steht sie nach davor
so wollen wir da uns wieder sehen
bei der Lanterne wollen wir stehen
wie einst Lili Marlen.

Unsere beide Schatten sahen wir einer aus
daß wir so lieb uns hatten
daß gleich man daraus
und alle Leute sollen es sehen
wie einst Lili Marlen.

Schon rief der Posten, sie blasen zap
fenstreich es kann drei Tage kosten
Kamrad, ich komm so gleich
da sagten wir auf wiedersehen
wie gerne wollt ich mit dir gehen
mit dir Lili Marlen.

Deine Schritte kennt sie, deine Zierengang
alle abend brennt sie,
doch mich vergaß sie lang
und sollten mir ein leids geschehen
wer wird bei der Lanterne stehen
mit dir Lili Marlen?

Aus dem Stillen raume, aus der erder Grund
heßt mich wie un Traüme
dein verliebster Mund
wenn sich die Spaten nebel drehn
werd'ich bei der Lanterne stehen
wie einst Lili Marlen.

The immense popularity of the German version led to a hurried English version done by Tommie Connor and broadcast by the BBC for the Allied troops. Eventually, both sides began broadcasting the song in both versions, interspersed with propaganda nuggets. The German singer was Lale Andersen, but it was immortalised when the anti-Nazi German, Marlene Dietrich began to sing it in 1943.

113

Above: Marlene Dietrich became associated with the song 'Lili Marlene'.

Liberation of Paris

On 7 August General von Choltitz had been made Military Governor of Paris, and on 21 August received instructions from Hitler ending with, "Paris must only fall into enemy hands as a heap of rubble". Von Choltitz had a reputation for unquestioning obedience to orders but thought this instruction would be self-defeating rather than sound strategy. On 19 August Von Choltitz, encouraged by the Swedish Consul General Raoul Nording, agreed to a cease-fire between the garrison and the Resistance.

The End of Japanese Domination

1944 was to mark a major turning point for the Allied armies in Burma after the disasters of 1942–43. Significant changes in the Allied Command structure in South East Asia brought about a new military organisation.

Balkans

In 1944 the Red Army burst into the Balkans causing Axis allies to begin switching sides whilst guerilla leaders jockeyed for position in preparation for the end of the war and seizing power. These groups were used as pawns by the Powers in a greater political game.

Arnhem – Operation Market Garden

By the autumn of 1944 all the Allied Commanders were frustrated by the lack of progress into Germany, following the initial successes after the landings in Normandy. On 10 September 1944 "Operation Market Garden" was revealed and approved: the Anglo–US 1st Airborne Army was to be dropped at points along the road from Eindhoven to Arnhem. Major General Robert Urquhart was put in command of the British 1st Airborne Division, whose task it was to capture the three most northerly bridges at Arnhem.

The Battle of The Bulge

On 16 September 1944 Hitler held a meeting with his generals in his underground headquarters in East Prussia, the "Wolf's Lair". General Jodl expressed concern that the advancing Americans might break through into Germany via the woods and hills of the Ardennes. Hitler's response was that he had already decided an offensive should be made from the Ardennes with the object of taking Antwerp.

114

The Films of 1944

Aventure Malgache – Alfred Hitchcock
Arsenic and Old Lace – Frank Capra
Black Magic (Charlie Chan Mystery) – Phil Rosen
Bon Voyage – Alfred Hitchcock
A Canterbury Tale – Michael Powell and Emeric Pressburger
Chinese Cat (Charlie Chan Mystery)– Phil Rosen
For Whom the Bell Tolls – Sam Wood
Gaslight – George Cukor
Go Down Death – Spencer Williams
Going My Way – Leo McCarey
Great Moment – Preston Sturges
Hail the Conquering Hero – Preston Sturges
Hairy Ape – Alfred Santell
Henry V – Laurence Olivier
Hollywood Canteen – Delmer Daves
Jane Eyre – Robert Stevenson
Mask of Dimitrios – Jean Negulesco
Meet Me in St Louis – Vincente Minnelli
Ministry of Fear – Fritz Lang
Murder My Sweet – Edward Dmytryk
Since You Went Away – John Cromwell
Thirty Seconds Over Tokyo – Mervyn LeRoy
Three Caballeros/Saludos Amigos – Walt Disney

HENRY V

Written by Shakespeare

Once more into the breach,
dear friends, once more;
Or close the wall up with
our English dead!
In peace there's nothing so
becomes a man
As modest stillness and humility;
But when the blast of war
blows in our ears,

Then imitate the action of the tiger...
On, on, you noblest English
Whose blood is fet from
fathers of war-proof –
Fathers that like so many Alexanders
Have in these parts from morn
till even fought...
Dishonour not your mothers; now attest
That those to whom you called
fathers did beget you...
I see you stand like greyhounds
in the slips,
Straining upon the start.
The game's afoot;
Follow your spirit; and upon this charge
Cry "God for Harry, England and
St George!

THERE'LL ALWAYS BE AN ENGLAND

Written by Parker and Charles

I give you a toast, ladies and gentlemen.
I give you a toast, ladies and gentlemen.
May this fair dear land we love so well
In dignity and freedom dwell.
Though worlds may change and go awry
While there is still one voice to cry –

There'll always be an England
While there's a country lane,
Wherever there's a cottage small
Beside a field of grain.
There'll always be an England
While there's a busy street,
Wherever there's a turning wheel,
A million marching feet.

Red, white and blue; what does it
mean to you?
Surely you're proud, shout it aloud,
"Britons, awake!"
The empire, too, we can depend on you.
Freedom remains. These are the chains
Nothing can break.

There'll always be an England,
And England shall be free,
If England means as much to you
As England means to me.

There'll Always Be An England', was premiered in the film *Discoveries*, based on Carol Levis's popular radio show. It was sung by a Welsh boy soprano called Glyn Davies. He was dressed in a midshipman's uniform and surrounded by an enormous chorus of bell-bottomed sailors. Within two months of the declaration of war, 200,000 copies of the sheet music had been sold and its popularity continued until the end of the war and even to this day with its echoes of defiance it is still sung as a rousing flag-waving chorus at patriotic occassions.

The Yalta Conference

On 4 February 1945, the big three Allied leaders, Stalin, Churchill and Roosevelt, met in Yalta in the Crimea to settle the future of Europe as soon as Germany was defeated. Roosevelt, who became increasingly unwell, met Churchill two days earlier at Malta before flying on to Yalta.

The Potsdam Conference

The conference held at Potsdam outside Berlin between 17 July and 2 August 1945, was the last of the Allied conferences to be held. When Roosevelt died on 12 April he had been succeeded by Harry S. Truman who announced on 24 July he had a new and powerful weapon to be used against Japan (the atomic bomb). The conference was in recess between 25 and 28 July due to the general election in Britain. Churchill suffered

116

man contributed more songs than any one else and many of his lyrics have been featured in this book. His name was Noel Gay.

Noel Gay

Noel Gay was born as Robert Armitage on 3 March 1898 in Wakefield, Yorkshire.

Gay was a child prodigy. Educated at the Wakefield Cathedral School, he often deputised for the cathedral organist. Starting in 1913, he began his studies at London's Royal College of Music. He completed four years of study for his BA and B.Mus degrees at Christ's Church College, Cambridge, and then became music director and organist at the St Anne's Church in London's Soho.

He might have been destined for a career in a university or a cathedral but, while attending Cambridge, his interest in musical comedy was awakened and he began to write popular songs. He contributed some material to the *Stop Press* revue, after which his career blossomed when he was commissioned to write the score for the *Charlot Show of 1926*. He was also the principal composer for still another show called *Clowns In Clover*, which starred Cecily Courtneidge and Jack Hulbert. It was around this time that he took the stage name of Noel Gay, to avoid embarrassing the church authorities.

an overwhelming defeat and was replaced by Clement Attlee who joined the conference on 28 July. Stalin was the only war leader left.

All through the war years, the theatres in London continued to mount productions. Although many of the theatres were bombed out, the shows kept on going. One

117

During the 1930s, Gay wrote complete scores and also contributed to shows, including:

For Andre Charlot's revue *Folly To Be Wise*, 'The King's Horses' (in collaboration with Harry Graham)
His first musical show, *Hold My Hand* (1931 in collaboration with lyricist Desmond Carter). Songs included:
'Pied Piper'
'What's In A Kiss'
'Hold My Hand'
'Turn On The Music'.

Other 1930s shows that Gay scored included:
She Couldn't Say No
That's A Pretty Thing
Jack O' Diamonds
Love Laughs!
O-Kay For Sound, the first of the famous Crazy Gang music-hall revues at the London Palladium. This play had the hit song 'The Fleet's In Port Again', a Bud Flanagan vocal.
Wild Oats
Me and My Girl (1937), the book and lyrics by L. Arthur Rose. This show featured the hit song 'The Lambeth Walk'. When the show was filmed in 1929, the film was called *The Lambeth Walk*.
The Little Dog Laughed (1939), another Crazy Gang revue.
'Run, Rabbit, Run' was the hit song, again sung by Bud Flanagan.

In the 1940s, Gay wrote for shows with lyrics mostly by Frank Eyton, including:

Light's Up (Let The People Sing), featuring 'Only A Glass of Champagne' and 'You've Done Something To My Heart"
Present Arms
La-Di-Di-Di-Da
The Love Racket
Meet Me Victoria
Sweetheart Mine
Bob's Your Uncle (1948)

His songs for films include for *Me And Marlborough*:
'All For A Shilling A Day'
'There's Something About A Soldier', Cicely Courtneidge vocal.
For *Feather Your Nest*, the song:
'Leaning On A Lamp Post', George Formby vocal.
For *The Camels Are Coming*, the song:
'Who's Been Polishing The Sun', Jack Hulbert vocal.
For *Sleepless Nights*, the song:
'I Don't Want To Go To Bed', Lupino Lane vocal.
For *Sailors Three*, the song:
'All Over The Place'.
Gay also composed 'Tondeleyo' for the film *White Cargo* (starring Hedy Lamarr). It has been reported that this was the first song synchronised into a British talking picture.

Some of the many other songs Gay composed are:

'All For The Love Of A Lady'
'Are We Downhearted? No!'
'Happy Days, Happy Months'
'Hey Little Hen'
'I Took My Harp To A Party' – Gracie Fields hit vocal.
'I'll Always Love You'
'Just A Little Fond Affection'
'Let's Have A Tiddley At the Milk Bar'
'Love Makes The World Go Round'
'Me And My Girl'
'My Thanks To You' (co-written with Norman Newell)
'Red, White and Blue'
'Round The Marble Arch'
'The Birthday of the Little Princess'
'The Girl Who Loves A Soldier'
'The Moment I Saw You', lyric Gordon Clifford
'The Moon Remembered, But You Forgot'
'When Alice Blue Gown Met Little Boy Blue'

In the 1950s, Gay was mostly inactive, writing little apart from 'I Was Much Better Off In The Army' and 'You Smile At Everyone But Me'. Gay had been going deaf for some years and now had to wear a hearing aid. He died on his birthday in 1954.

Gay had formed a publishing company in 1938 – Noel Gay Music – and after his death in 1954 his son, Richard Armitage (born 12 August 1928, Wakefield, died 17 November 1986), took over the company and published one more Noel Gay song 'Love Me Now'. Richard expanded and developed the company into one of the largest television and talent agencies in Europe.

London Shows During The War

Alice in Wonderland & Through the Looking Glass, Apple Sauce, Arc de Triomphe, Artists & Models, Best Bib and Tucker, Big Top, Black Vanities, Blossom Time, Come Out Of Your Shell, Come Out to Play, Diversion, Diversion No. 2, Dubarry Was a Lady, Fine and Dandy, Full Swing, Fun and Games, Funny Side Up, Gangway, Get a Load of This, Happidrome, Happy Birthday, Hi-De-Hi, It's Time to Dance, Jenny Jones, La-Di-Da-Di-Da, Lady Behave, Let's Face It, Light and Shade, Lights Up, Lisbon Story, Meet Me Victoria, More New Faces, New Ambassadors Revue, New Faces, Nineteen-Naughty-One, Old Chelsea, Orchids and Onions, Panama Hattie, Present Arms, Rise Above It, Scoop, Silver Patrol, Six Pairs of Shoes, Skirts, Sky High, Something for the Boys, Something in the Air, Strike a New Note, Strike Up the Music, Sunny River, Susie, Sweet and Low, Sweeter and Lower, Swinging the Gate, The Knight Was Bold, The Love Racket, This is the Army, Top of the World, Up and Doing, Waltz Without End, Wild Rose

The Films of 1945

Boy! What a Girl – Arthur Leonard
Caesar and Cleopatra – Gabriel Pascal
Conflict – Curtis Bernhardt
Corn is Green – Irving Rapper
Ivan the Terrible: Part I: Ivan Groznyi – Sergei Eisenstein
Lady on a Train – Charles David
Lost Weekend – Billy Wilder
Men Who Tread on the Tiger's Tale – Akira Kurosawa
Mildred Pierce – Michael Curtiz
Objective Burma! – Raoul Walsh
Open City (Roma, Citta Aperta) – Roberto Rossellini
Picture of Dorian Gray – Albert Lewin
Scarlet Street – Fritz Lang
Southerner – Jean Renoir
Spellbound – Alfred Hitchcock
State Fair – Walter Lang
Story of G.I. Joe – William Wellman
Strange Affair of Uncle Harry – Robert Siodmak
Detour – Edgar G. Ulmer
They Were Expendable – John Ford
To Have and Have Not – Howard Hawks

The Battle for Berlin

Much has been said and written about the fall of Berlin at the end of the war. Many have argued that the Anglo-American forces should have made the taking of Berlin a primary objective rather than leaving it to the Soviet forces to take the German capital. However, many forget that the Allied agreement at the Yalta conference in February 1945 promised that the Anglo-American forces would halt at the Elbe. The Americans became obsessed with the idea that the Nazis would make a final stand in Bavaria.

On Tuesday 8 May 1945 Winston Churchill broadcast to the nation and the Empire:

"The evil doers are now prostrate before us. Our gratitude to our splendid allies goes forth from all our hearts in this island and throughout the British Empire."

Once the news had been broadcast that the war was over then 8 May 1945 was declared a public holiday. After five years and eight months of war in Europe Nazi Germany surrendered.

Victory in Japan

On 6 August 1945, the first atomic bomb was dropped on the Japanese city of Hiroshima. That devastating event killed between 60,000 and 80,000 people, either immediately or in the weeks directly after the explosion. Another 70,000 suffered horrendous injuries. The long-term genetic effects on the surviving population are still not fully understood. On 9 August of that same year, a second attack, with a similar device wrought havoc on the city of Nagasaki.

WORLD WAR II, 1939-1945

On 8 August Russia honoured her part of the agreement by entering the Japanese war as soon as the conflict against Germany was over. Their vast war machine moved into Manchuria. By 14 August, the Japanese Emperor had unconditionally surrendered, in the face of the potential destruction of his country. On 30 August a contingent of American and British troops landed at Yokusuka. Many Japanese officers could not accept what was happening and chose the honourable way out by committing suicide.

World War II was now finally over. Flags and bunting lined the streets of every town and village across the country. Everyone was celebrating in the streets, still singing the songs that had kept them going during the five and a half years of darkness.

A debt is owed to the singers, songwriters, musicians and entertainers who boosted the morale of the troops and civilians through every phase of the worst wars the world has ever seen.

During World War II the Allied powers (Britain, France, *USA et al.*) lost over 16.5 million and the Axis powers (Germany and Japan *et al.*) lost over six million military personnel.

121

Epilogue

WHEN THIS BLOODY WAR IS OVER

When this bloody war is over
No more soldiering for me.
When I get my civvy clothes on
Oh, how happy I shall be!
No more church parades on Sunday
No more putting in for leave.
I shall kiss the Sergeant-Major
How I'll miss him; how he'll grieve.

Above: The heroes return.

Appendix

Popular Songs Of World War I

'A Khaki Lad' – Reinald Werrenrath had the big vocal.

'All of No Man's Land is Ours' – James Reese Europe's Hellfighters.

'America Here's My Boy' – The Peerless Quartet's hit.

'America, I Love You' – Edgar Leslie lyric and Archie Gottlier music.

'And He'd Say "Oo-La-La Wee-Wee"' – this Harry Ruby and George Jessel (1919) tune was a big hit for Billy Murray (and others).

'Beside a Belgian Water Tank'

'But for Gawd's Sake Don't Send Me'

'Coast Artillery Song'

'Come On and Join'

'Charlotte the Harlot'

'Darktown Strutters Ball, The'

'Don't Bite The Hand That's Feeding You'

'Don't Cry Frenchy, Don't Cry' – this duet by Charles Hart/Elliott Shaw was a hit.

'Give Me A Kiss By the Numbers'

'Goodbye Dolly'

'Goodbye Jenny'

'Good-Bye, Good Luck, God Bless You'

'Good Morning Mr Zip Zip Zip' – this Bollaert/Rob't Lloyd tune was a vocal for Arthur Fields.

'Hail! Hail! The Gang's All Here!'

'Have A Little Regiment of Your Own'

'Hitchy Koo'

'Homeward Bound'

'I Ain't got Weary Yet!'

'I Didn't Raise My Boy to be a Soldier' – this anti-war song was a vocal hit for Morton Harvey.

'I Don't Know Where I'm Going But I'm On My Way'

'I Don't Want to Get Well' – a Van and Schenck comedy duet.

'I Want to Go Home'

'If I'm Not at the Roll-Call'

'I'd Feel at Home If They'd Let Me Join the Army' – a Billy Murray vocal hit.

'I'll Make a Man of You'

'I'll Come Back to You When It's All Over' – another Arthur Fields vocal.

'It's A Long, Long Way to the USA and the Girl I Left Behind' – this Jack Judge and Harry Williams tune was composed two years before WWI began, but was popular with the soldiers of Britain and America.

'JA-DA' – this Arthur Fields hit release is still a popular Dixieland tune. McCormick's version was the big hit. Lena Ford lyrics, with Ivor Novello music.

'Lafayette We Hear You Calling' – a hit for Reinald Werrenrath.

'Li'l Liza Jane'

'Look At the Ears on Him'

'Mademoiselle From Armentieres'

'My Belgian Rose' – words and music by George Benoit, Robert Levenson and Ted Garton A WW1 "war bride" song!

'My Buddy'

'Never Forget to Write Home' – sung by the great Irving Kaufman.

'Oh! How I Hate To Get Up In The Morning' – words and music by Irving Berlin (1918).

'Oh It's a Lovely War' – J. P. Long and Maurice Scott

'Oui Oui Marie' – yet another Arthur Fields hit.

'Our Country's In It Now' – the Orpheus Quartet.

'Pay-Day!'

'Roarious'
'Round Her Neck She Wears A Yeller Ribbon'
'Save Your Kisses 'Til the Boys Come Home'
'Sims's Flotilla'
'Sister Susie's Sewing Shirts for Soldiers' – a huge hit vocal for Al Jolson. R.P. Weston lyrics with Hermann E. Darewski music.
'Song of the Officers' Torpedo Class'
'Soup Song'
'Stand, Stand Up America'
'Take Me Back to Dear Old Blighty'
'The Army Bean'
'The Battle Song of Liberty'
'The Last Long Mile'
'The Old Grey Mare' – the Collins and Harlan duet was a big hit.
'The Rose of No Man's Land', Charles Hart and Elliott Shaw vocal duet hit.
'The Sunshine of Your Smile'
'The Worst Is Yet to Come' – a hit for the Peerless Quartet.
'There'll Be A Hot Time in the Old Town Tonight' – while Arthur Fields and the Peerless Quartet had a WW1 hit with this tune, it was originally heard in Babe Connor's bagnio in St Louis, Missouri.
'There's A Long, Long Trail' – composed by Stoddard King and Zo Elliott.
'They'll Be Mighty Proud in Dixie of Their Old Black Joe' – performed by Campbell and Burr.
'Till We Meet Again – Raymond B. Egan lyrics and Richard Whiting music. This song was the last best-selling sheet music; five million copies were sold within the first year.
'Torpedo Jim'
'The Countersigns'
'Uncle Sam'

'We're All Going Calling on the Kaiser' – a hit for Arthur Fields and the Peerless Quartet.
'We Don't Want to Lose You'
'We're Going Over'
'When Pershing's Men Go Marching Into Picardy'
'When Yankee Doodle Learns to Parlez Vous Français' – still another Arthur Fields vocal hit.
'When You Wore A Tulip'
'When Belgium put the Kibosh on the Kaiser'
'Where They Were'
'Would You Rather Be A Colonel With An Eagle On Your Shoulder, Or A Private With A Chicken On Your Knee?' – Sidney Mitchell/Archie Gottlieb tune, heard 20 years later in WWII.
'You'll Be There'
'Your Boy Is On The Coal Pile Now'

Popular Songs Of World War II

'A Lovely Way To Spend An Evening'
'Ac-cent-tchu-ate The Positive' – Johnny Mercer hit vocal.
'Amapola', Jimmy Dorsey Orchestra, Bob Eberle and Helen O'Connell vocal.
'As Time Goes By' – Dooley Wilson vocal (soundtrack: *Casablanca*).
'Auf Wiedersehen Sweetheart' – Vera Lynn vocal.
'Coming In On A Wing And A Prayer' – The Song Spinners.
'Deep In The Heart of Texas' – Johnny Mercer vocal.
'Don't Get Around Much Anymore (aka: Never No Lament)' – Duke Ellington Orchestra.
'Do Nothing Till You Hear From Me'– Duke Ellington Orchestra.
'Elmer's Tune', Glenn Miller Orchestra.
'G. I. Jive' – Johnny Mercer vocal.

APPENDIX

'Idaho' – Benny Goodman Orchestra.
'Juke Box Saturday Night' – Glenn Miller
Orchestra.
'I Can't Begin To Tell You' – Sammy Kaye
Orchestra.
'(If They Asked Me) I Could Write A Book',
'I Don't Want To Walk Without You, Baby',
'I Know Why and So Do You'
'I've Heard That Song Before'
'I Left My Heart At The Stage Door Canteen' –
Sammy Kaye Orchestra.
'I'll Be With You In Apple Blossom Time' – The
Andrews Sisters vocal.
'I'll Buy That Dream'– Helen Forrest and Dick
Haymes vocal.
'I'll Get By (As Long As I Have You)'– Harry
James Orchestra with Dick Haymes vocal.
'I'll Never Smile Again' – Frank Sinatra and the
Pied Pipers.
'I'll Walk Alone' – Dinah Shore vocal.
'I'm Making Believe' – The Ink Spots vocal.
'In The Führer's Face' – Spike Jones Orchestra.
'Is You Is Or Is You Ain't My Baby' – Louis
Jordan Orchestra and vocal.
'It Might As Well Be Spring' – Paul Weston
Orchestra, with Margaret Whiting vocal.
'It's Been A Long Long Time' – Charlie Spivak
with Irene Day vocal.
'Long Ago and Far Away' – Jo Stafford vocal hit.
'Maria Elena' – Jimmy Dorsey Orchestra, with
Bob Eberly vocal.
'Moonlight Becomes You' – Bing Crosby vocal.
'Mr Five By Five' – Freddie Slack Orchestra, with
Ella Mae Morse vocal.
'My Devotion' – Vaughn Monroe Orchestra.
'My Shining Hour'
'Ole Buttermilk Sky' – Kay Kyser Orchestra.

'On The Atchison, Topeka, and Santa Fe' –
Johnny Mercer hit vocal.
'One Dozen Roses' – Harry James Orchestra.
'Paper Doll' – The Mills Brothers vocal.
'Roll Out The Barrel'
'San Fernando Valley' – Roy Rogers vocal.
'Saturday Night Is The Loneliest Night of The
Week'
'Sentimental Journey' – Les Brown Orchestra.
'Sleepy Lagoon' – Harry James had the big hit.
'Speak Low (When You Speak Love)'
'Spring Will Be A Little Late This Year' – Deanna
Durbin vocal.
'Stardust' – Frank Sinatra and the Pied Pipers.
'Sunday, Monday and Always' – Bing Crosby
vocal hit.
'Sunrise Serenade' – Glenn Miller Orchestra.
'Take The "A" Train' – Duke Ellington Orchestra.
'Temptation' – Perry Como vocal.
'The Last Time I Saw Paris'
'The Very Thought Of You' – Vaughn Monroe
Orchestra.
'There I've Said It Again' – Vaughn Monroe
Orchestra.
'They're Either Too Young or Too Old' – Betty
Davis hit vocal.
'Till Then' – Mills Brothers vocal.
'To Each His Own' – Eddy Howard vocal.
'You Always Hurt The One You Love' – Sammy
Kaye Orchestra.
'You Belong To My Heart' – Charlie Spivak
Orchestra.
'You'd Be So Nice To Come Home To',
'You'll Never Know' – Dick Haymes vocal.
'Yours' – Jimmy Dorsey Orchestra.

Index

INDEX